FUN IN MONTREAL

Titles in the series

Acapulco
Bahamas
London
Montreal
Puerto Rico
San Francisco
St. Martin
Waikiki

FODOR'S
FUN IN
MONTREAL

Ira Mayer

Published by
FODOR'S TRAVEL GUIDES
New York

Copyright © 1985 by Fodor's Travel Guides

No part of this book may be reproduced in any form without permission in writing from the publisher.

ISBN 0-679-01168-4

Maps and plans by Burmar
Illustration by Ted Burwell

MANUFACTURED IN THE UNITED STATES OF AMERICA
10 9 8 7 6 5 4 3 2 1

Contents

General Information	7
Overview	14
Getting Around	24
Downtown	27
(Includes selection of Downtown hotels and some restaurants)	
Old Montreal	50
(Includes some restaurants)	
St. Denis and Prince Arthur	63
(Includes selection of area hotels and some restaurants)	
Other City Excursions	73
(Includes some restaurants)	
Shopping	80
Restaurants	87
Night Life	102
Daytrips	109
(Includes selection of area accommodations and restaurants)	
Quebec City and Daytrips	116
(Includes selections of city and area hotels and restaurants)	

Maps and Plans

Montreal	16
The Metro	25

CONTENTS 6

Downtown Montreal	28
Old Montreal	52
St. Denis	64
Outside Montreal	110
Downtown Quebec City	118
Laurentians Area	126

General Information

Montreal is a year-round city of culture and activity. Winters offer cross-country skiing in the city's own Mount Royal Park and downhill and cross-country skiing within an hour's drive in such Laurentian resorts as Mont Tremblant and Val David. The heated "Underground City," linked by Métro stops, makes it possible to shop, dine, attend concerts and recitals, and even make it back to certain hotels without once having to face the cold. The winters can be brutal, though if truth be known the early 1980s found them tame and snowless. Temperatures are generally well below freezing December through February. The museums, restaurants, and other indoor attractions will still hold, with the concert, ballet, and opera seasons in full swing. But if skiing is part of your itinerary, don't make plans too far ahead, and keep in mind that reservations *are* a must when the snow becomes good.

Spring finds the Botanical Gardens beginning to

bloom outdoors as well as in the nine greenhouses on the grounds. You can expect temperatures to inch up to the 40s and 50s, though you'll want some nice heavy sweaters for cool surprises. Summer heats up dramatically, but is usually comfortable even when the thermometer closes in on 90 degrees. Evenings are still pleasant, the harbor cruises offering cool-water breezes. There are wind surfing on Ile Notre Dame, peddle boats in Parc Fontaine, and picnics to be dined on in Mount Royal Park. Cultural activities move outdoors—often in the way of free concerts, drama, and children's shows in public parks. A pamphlet published each spring by the Tourist Bureau lists some 300 such events. The Grand Prix auto race takes place in Montreal in early June, followed by the Montreal Jazz Festival in July and the International Film Festival in August; Quebec City is host to a winter *carnivale* in February and *Festival d'Été* in July.

The turning maple leaves make fall spectacular—cool and dry, with Mount Royal a wildly colorful backdrop over the city. This is when *calèche* (horse-drawn carriage) rides are most inviting. A wool blanket provided by the driver keeps you warm as you're drawn through the streets of Old Montreal or down Rue Sherbrooke or around Mount Royal Park.

The seasons come a little quicker, and the air is a few degrees cooler, in the Laurentian mountains and Quebec City.

What to Pack

Montreal is so clean that you'll quickly realize neatness counts over style. Indeed, the city can be as formal or informal as you make it. Apart from the Ritz-Carlton, where jackets and ties for men are mandatory even at the Café de Paris Bar, and perhaps at a handful of old-line restaurants, even top-flight establishments will accommodate any and all comers who are reasonably attired. Most people dining in the best spots do dress up, though, as much to make a night of it for themselves as for any other reason.

Winters are somewhat more sedate in this sense, especially if you're attending a performance at one of the halls at Place des Arts, when everyone's decked out in their finest. But in summer, just about anything goes—from clean jeans and a golf shirt to business suits for men, from casual slacks or skirt with blouse to silk dresses for women.

Those who frequent the singles bars and clubs in a former "English" section along Crescent, Montagne, Bishop, and Mackay Streets tend to be very fashion conscious. This is less the case in what used to be called the "French" section along upper St. Denis and in the Prince Arthur/Duluth districts, where the populace is more of the young marrieds and/or artsy variety. Lower St. Denis, where the older teens and young 20s hang out, is for the jeans-and-T-shirt and leather-jacket set. Old Montreal has a little of everything: artists and craftspeople who look the part, living in spacious lofts and frequenting local bistros, and young executives who look *their* part at some of Montreal's most tradition-minded restaurants.

Swimming is available indoors and/or outdoors at many hotels and for a small locker charge at Olympic Park all year round (outdoors at Ile St. Helene in summer), so bring trunks or a swimsuit. Comfortable shoes are always in order—women who wear heels will want to keep in mind that Old Montreal has cobblestone streets. Boots or high shoes with good traction are in order for winter, along with clothes that insulate: as with skiers, layers that can be peeled off or added to as you move about will work best. Skiers themselves will probably want to bring their own gear, though rentals are widely available in season.

The Laurentian ski resorts have their own codes, which tend to be more fashionable at the larger places, more relaxed at the inns and *auberges*. Much as in Montreal, it depends on which resorts you go to as to how dressy the evenings get and how decked out the skiers are. Quebec City pretty much parallels Montreal as far as fashion goes, though jackets and ties are a little more the norm in better restaurants. There's less of a jet-set air here too.

Trip Tips

Montreal is served by two airports: Dorval for flights entering from North America (including other points in Canada) and Mexico, and Mirabel for those arriving from other continents. Bus service from Dorval is $5 to downtown, with stops at several of the major hotels. From these points you can always catch the Métro or a bus or cab to other places. A metered cab from Dorval will run about $15 before tip, and private limousines cost $18, regardless of the number of passengers. Budget travelers should note that People Express flies into Burlington, Vermont, from various points in the northeast U.S. Bus service leaves regularly from the Burlington Airport for downtown Montreal. The trip takes about 1½ hours but can represent savings as much as 50% over direct flight.

Those driving to Montreal can pick up Trans Canada Highway 15 from such major U.S. arteries as Interstates 87 and 89, or can take Canada 55 and Canada 10 from Interstate 91. These are excellently marked roadways—as are those in Montreal itself. Distances and speeds are posted in kilometers, not miles. Gasoline is sold in Imperial gallons, which are equivalent to 1.2 U.S. gallons. Lead-free gasoline is labeled *sans plomb;* oil is *huile. Service libre* means self service—not free service.

Do watch for parking regulations: much of downtown Montreal (as well as Quebec City) is off-limits for on-the-street parking during the week. Other areas are restricted during certain hours on given days of the week. Signs are clearly posted—but in French only. Most hotels offer parking (sometimes free, sometimes

GENERAL INFORMATION

not) and the excellent public transportation available makes it most inviting not to bother with a car.

Entering Montreal by rail from the U.S. is a matter of connecting with one of Amtrak's two services from Washington, D.C., and New York. From New York this is a 12-hour trip by night, nine hours by day; add about three hours for the stretch between Washington and New York. Montreal is also served domestically by the national VIA Rail service from most major cities (514–871–1331).

Terminus Voyageur (514–842–2281), atop the Berri-de-Montigny Métro station, is the city's primary bus terminal. Greyhound runs from New York to Montreal in eight hours, Vermont Transit from Boston in seven hours.

Both the Laurentians and Quebec City can be reached by auto, bus, and rail—the latter about a three-hour ride away, assuming passable road conditions during the winter months.

Miscellaneous information: Quebec Province is in the Eastern Time zone and observes Daylight Savings Time; clocks move one hour forward in the spring and one hour back in the fall.

The City of Montreal Commission on Initiative and Economic Development (CIDEM) publishes a pamphlet titled "Useful Information for the Handicapped" that covers most essential facts. Available free by mail from CIDEM-Tourisme, 155 Notre Dame St. East, Montreal H2Y 1B5.

Money

At press time, U.S. dollars are worth about 30% more than their Canadian counterparts! This makes traveling in Canada particularly advantageous for American citizens, since prices as quoted in Canadian dollars are roughly the same numerically as (or already a bit lower than) those in the U.S. in U.S. dollars. Spending $50

GENERAL INFORMATION 12

for two on dinner thus comes out to about $35. And what you get for your money even at $50 almost always represents excellent value.

Currency can be changed at bank-operated kiosks at air, rail, and bus terminals on weekends as well as during business hours. The cashiers at all bank branches will also convert U.S. to Canadian dollars. Currency is based on the same decimal system as in the U.S.—but beware that $2 bills, which have never been popular in the U.S., are common in Canada.

Most hotels and restaurants will also convert money for you, but usually at rates below those offered by banks; major credit cards use the rate in effect on the date of the transaction. When traveling it is always advisable to carry travelers' checks, which are insured against loss, rather than hard currency. Credit cards are accepted just about everywhere a tourist might go around Montreal and Quebec City, with American Express, Visa, and MasterCard almost universally recognized.

Entry and Customs

U.S. citizens need only proof of birth date and identity, not necessarily a passport, in order to enter Canada and re-enter the U.S. A driver's license, voter registration card, or birth certificate will do. No visa is required. An oral declaration of the purpose of your visit (usually "vacation" will suffice) and whether you are carrying tobacco or alcohol products is pretty much all that's required. Firearms, meats, and pets can present difficulties in an otherwise simple situation.

Travelers under the age of 19 require written permission of a parent or guardian specifying length of stay as well as the above-mentioned proof of identity.

Upon returning home, those who have been out of the U.S. for 36 hours or more are entitled to bring in up to $400 per person duty free, including 200

GENERAL INFORMATION

cigarets, 50 non-Cuban cigars, and one liter of alcohol. Art and antiques may be brought in duty free in any amount.

Important note: when reentering the U.S. by air from Canada, you clear Customs at the point of departure in Canada—not upon arrival in the U.S. Leave time (an extra 20 minutes or half hour unless you're bringing a major chunk of Canada home with you) when heading to the airport.

Overview

From the top of Mount Royal, 764 feet above sea level, the island of Montreal is a larger-than-life panorama. The mountain stands at the center of the island, with Victorian fieldstone houses and glittering steel-and-concrete skyscrapers side by side at its feet. South, the Green Mountains of Vermont loom on the horizon. Moving from the horizon back toward the Mount, the St. Lawrence Seaway can be seen cutting its southwest to northeast way 1,100 miles into the North American continent; the Islands of St. Helene and Notre Dame float at its center, housing the remains of Expo '67. The main parts of the city lie between the Mount at the north and the river at the south. Just about within arm's reach from the lookout point are McGill University, Place Ville Marie (behind which is the port of Old Montreal), and the first-class shops, museums, and office buildings of Sherbrooke Street.

A second lookout point a few hundred yards eastward takes in the Olympic Park, the Botanical Gardens, and the posh French-dominated neighborhood of Outremont. The road heading out to the west runs through Côte des Neiges, passing the University of Montreal and Saint Joseph's Oratory to the north and winding back toward downtown via another well-heeled center-city community, the Anglophile Westmount. (Montreal is comprised of 29 municipalities with a combined population of 1.8 million people and joined by the The Montreal Urban Community. Outremont, Westmount, and Côte des Neiges are among these municipalities.)

Mount Royal—so named by Jacques Cartier in 1535—is an excellent first stop for visitors, providing as it does a sense of the city's grandeur. Conversely, the mountain is visible from just about everywhere (except through skyscrapers, of course); with its 100-foot high cross and "devil's fork" broadcast tower, it's an excellent way to orient yourself. Once you get to the park via public bus or car, a small tram will carry you to the main lookout.

If the weather calls for other than an outdoor first view, try Altitude 737 at Place Ville-Marie—a restaurant and bar on the 41st floor of this distinctively cross-shaped tower—or the similar rooftop establishments at the Sheraton, Hyatt or Château Champlain Hotels. Drinks are the best bet in such places, though all offer menus that run upwards of $16 per person at lunch, and higher at dinner.

Another alternative that can help establish bearings in this highly industrial yet very cultured city is a Gray Line bus tour. The 2½ hour "Greater Montreal" tour ($10.00 for adults, $5.00 for children) essentially drives you past most of the main sights, stopping at Notre Dame Cathedral and Mount Royal and leaving you with enough of an impression to know which areas you want to cover in greater depth on your own. More extensive tours are available, but that time is better spent personalizing your visit. This is a city to be walked—and with an outstanding public transportation system to carry you between neighborhoods. (A second tour operator is Murray Hill, though its reputation is not as strong as Gray Line's.)

OVERVIEW *16*

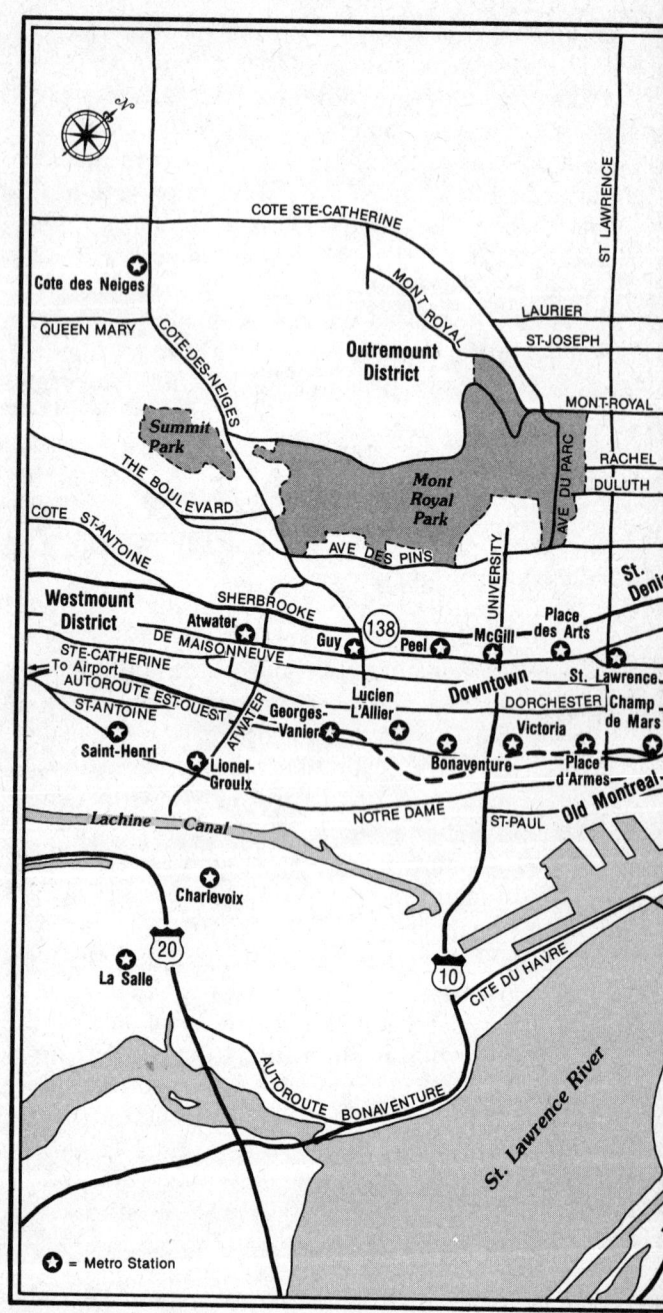

17 OVERVIEW

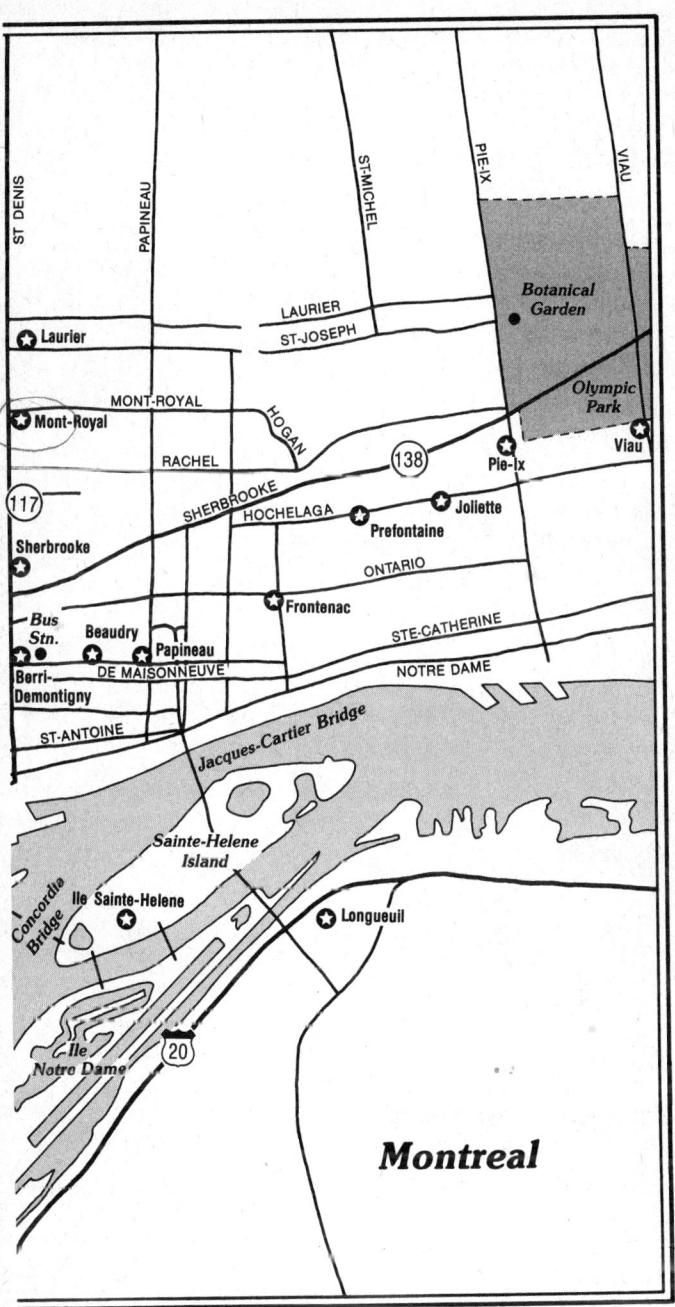

If Montreal is in many ways a series of distinct neighborhoods, it is also a city of high contrasts. Most prominent is the clash between French and English cultures. Quebec Province, the state in which Montreal lies, has a vociferous separatist movement that was fueled by the late French President Charles de Gaulle's fiery 1967 proclamation, "Vive le Quebec libre!"—a call for the liberation of Quebec from the rest of Canada. Full secession was avoided by public vote in 1973, though other provinces must now adhere to strict regulations calling for all public signs to be in French as well as English. Ironically, in Quebec Province, French is often the only route chosen.

Visitors are not likely to be confronted by many Montrealers who don't speak at least some English, though that prospect increases as you travel into other areas in the province. Certainly restaurant and hotel personnel are almost always bilingual, and those who aren't invariably know where to find someone who is. The only real ticklish language barrier could be for drivers: "No Parking" zones are clearly marked as such by signs bearing little cars with a slash through them, but the days of the week indicated on those signs are in French only—with Montreal police especially quick with their ticket pads and tow trucks.

Those with no French background will pick up "menu French" easily enough just by comparing the offerings at a handful of places. Montreal restaurants are mandated to post their menus out front and most comply in both French and English. Still, it doesn't take long to catch on that "poisson" means fish, not poison, and "viande" means meat. The occasional men's *brasserie* (beer hall) may not welcome Anglophiles or tourists generally and will make that fact known by pretty much ignoring those who walk in. These also tend to be "men only" hangouts for card-playing and joke-telling; a few will have colorful signs proclaiming "bienvenue filles" or "women are welcome."

While neighborhoods were once very much

demarcated for French or English—St. Lawrence Boulevard, dividing the city for East and West addresses, once having been the "border," English to the west, French to the east—the population patterns have been shifting and there is greater integration among the two cultures than ever before, despite the 64% dominance of Francophiles in the Greater Montreal area. About 16% of the population is of Anglo-Saxon descent, with another 9% contributing to the English-speaking community. The remainder includes those of European, Middle-Eastern, and Asian heritage who, while they may have maintained strong cultural and linguistic ties to their homelands, have largely been assimilated by the city. While there is a Chinatown downtown, for example, only about 300 of the city's Chinese population of 25,000 live in it; most are spread throughout Montreal.

Aside from the primary Anglo/Franco cultural split, a second immediately striking contrast is that of old versus new. This is nowhere more apparent than with the Greystone and Alcan Buildings on Sherbrooke. Only a few blocks apart (the former at University Street, the latter between Stanley and Drummond) both are traditional stone houses on the outside. But while the façades have been kept intact, the insides have been gutted—with skyscrapers of aluminum-and-glass and concrete rising from inside them. The greystone houses facing on Sherbrooke were dismantled, brick by brick, the new buildings erected, and then the façades replaced!

Architectural and historical preservation groups have become active in recent years, but not quite soon enough to stave off some demolition and (apparently unneeded) reconstruction; Victorian mansions have been supplanted by high-tech office buildings despite the migration of many companies to Toronto following the separatist movement of the late 1960s and early 1970s.

The Highlights

Touring this dazzlingly clean and unusually safe city is best approached by taking it neighborhood by neighborhood. While each of the following areas is discussed in greater detail in individual chapters, this can serve as a general outline for structuring your visit:

Downtown is for shoppers and museum-goers—along Sherbrooke Street, which is Montreal's Fifth Avenue or Rodeo Drive—or in the famed Underground City, the seemingly endless boutique-filled caverns beneath the city's scores of office buildings. Most of these shopping centers are connected via the Métro.

With several hotels part of the underground network, winter visitors need never step into the cold, whether they're searching for designer clothes or looking for the finest restaurants (some in shopping malls!) or attending the opera, ballet, or symphony at Place des Arts. Downtown, too, are a number of major night-life strips, with numerous restaurants, bars, and discos—St. Catherine Street for teenagers; and Crescent, Montagne, Bishop, and Mackay Streets for singles in their late 20s and 30s.

Old Montreal (Vieux Montreal) is a day and night treat with its narrow, winding streets by the harbor and its architecture dating back as far as the seventeenth century. Place Jacques Cartier, named after the first "discoverer" of Montreal, is lined with restaurants and cafés. Horse-and-buggy rides, known as *calèche*, can be taken along the waterfront or through the main streets. Galleries, boutiques, nightclubs, and Notre Dame church are among other highlights, with many of Montreal's finest restaurants located in beautifully restored eighteenth-century mansions.

St. Denis is another big area for night life. In summer, its *terrasses* (outdoor cafés) south of Sherbrooke are overflowing with people in their late teens and early 20s. Northward, the crowd gets a little older, or at least dresses as though it is. Suddenly the jeans and T-shirts are replaced by business attire. Here the young couples and young executive types head toward Prince Arthur and Duluth Streets.

Prince Arthur is a pedestrian mall filled with street performers, mostly bring-your-own bottle Greek and Italian restaurants, bars, and dessert shops. Duluth is on its way to the same stature. When visiting during the day, take a stroll up St. Lawrence Boulevard, a unique conglomeration of old European and Oriental shops offset by the occasional modish boutique or coffeehouse.

Excursions within the city should take in **Olympic Park** and the **Botanical Gardens.** The 1976 Olympics may have cost the city $1 billion, and the maintaining of Olympic Park has been costing it an additional $5 million annually ever since. With its unfinished stadium—a would-be office tower hovers overhead—it does offer all comers year-round indoor swimming in at least three out of the six pools in the complex. Even more pleasant for strolling are the Botanical Gardens, with nine interconnected greenhouses as well as 200 acres of gardens.

La Ronde is an amusement park on the island of Ste. Helene, accessible by Métro. Just to the left of the entrance is the Montreal Aquarium—small but well stocked, and worth a quick tour.

Other possibilities include hour-long river cruises, riding the Lachine Rapids (via motorized or rubber rafts), "Man and His World" (the remains of Expo '67) on the man made island of Notre Dame and, of course, trips into the nearby countryside for everything from skiing to antique hunting to eating and hiking. Of special note: the auto racing classic Grand Prix takes place in early June on Ile Notre Dame.

You may very well want to build your stay in Montreal around meals. The city rightly stakes its claim to culinary excellence second only in North America to New York. French food is a staple, in cream-laden classic and lighter "nouvelle" modes. But there is also outstanding Vietnamese, Italian, Quebecoise (the local variation on French), East European, Indian, Greek, and Chinese food to be sampled, with seafood in this port city an almost universal specialty. Montrealers don't eat especially early, either, which helps make the case for making an evening of dining.

So called "businessmen's" lunches are especially popular and easy on the budget. First-class restaurants where you would expect to spend $30 or more for a three-course dinner *à la carte* (not counting drinks) will have daily luncheon specials for $6–$8, including appetizer and dessert, Mondays through Fridays. With a 25% liquor tax, another growing trend is the restaurant with a sign urging "Apportez votre vin"—Bring your own wine (or beer). This, too, helps to keep eating out at reasonable levels. Even so, you can dine well *and* inexpensively any time and in any district in Montreal, at top-name establishments with moderately priced *table d'hôte* dinners or at local restaurants with a specific ethnic bent.

There is a similarly broad range of accommodations available in Montreal. We will spotlight a selection of the best in every category, from the larger deluxe hotels, where service counterbalances the anonymity of size, to smaller hotels, inns (*auberges*), and other highly personalized lodging. Almost all of the places mentioned in the chapters to follow have special packages available for weekend visitors. These are usually at half the regular rate, with little or no extra charge for children. Be sure to check on the availability of such deals; they can give even the budget traveler access to the likes of the fashionable old-world Ritz-Carlton or the dynamically modern Four Seasons. Both Montreal and McGill Universities open their student apartments to tourists in summer.

Daytrips to the Laurentians are especially worthwhile for skiing in winter; swimming, boating, and hiking in summer; and observing the foliage in autumn. Similarly, Quebec City is only three hours away.

Here, the French influence is predominant in a city a tenth the size of Montreal but boasting some of the finest cuisine to be found in all Canada.

Getting Around

Montreal's Métro, or underground subway, is one of the world's most efficient and most pleasant public transportation systems. The trains on its four lines run frequently from about 6:00 A.M. until after 1:00 A.M. Connections are convenient and well marked, with free transfers between Métro and bus lines. The stations themselves are a joy, the entrances all designed by different artists. Some stations, such as Champ des Mars, are quite stunning with brightly colored stained glass. And they are reasonably priced, to boot: 80 cents per fare, or a book good for 16 rides (including all transfer privileges) for $11. Those planning an extended stay should consider a monthly pass for about $25—good for unlimited access to Métro and buses. (Bus fares are the same, and the ticket books and passes are good on both. On buses you must request a transfer if you wish to continue the trip on the Métro; this too is free.) If you wish to pay a single fare at the

25 GETTING AROUND

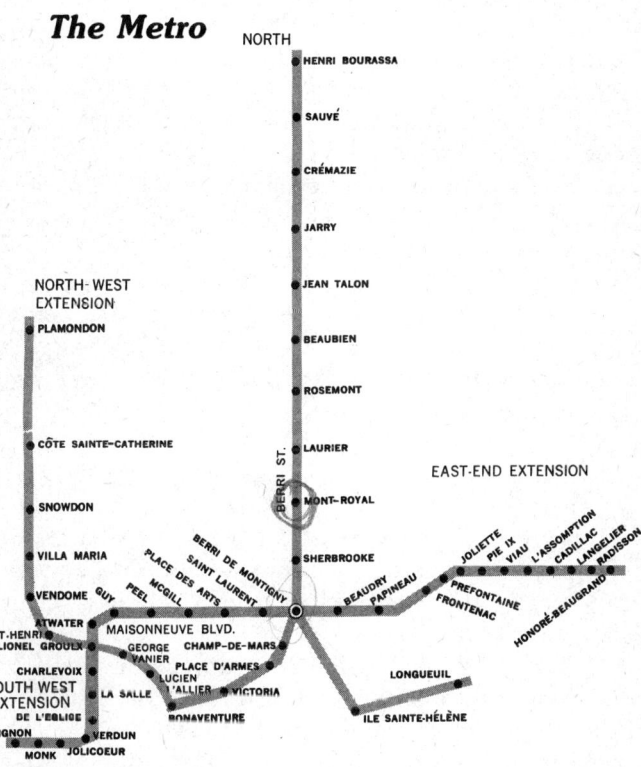

Métro, you drop your money into the chute at the manned booth; if you need change, the attendant will provide it. You must then still deposit your fare yourself into the chute; tickets are fed into a slot on the turnstile.

There are only two possibly confusing things to watch for relative to the Métro. First, the city map published by the Quebec government features all Métro stops prominently displayed in black. It does not, however, differentiate among the four interconnecting lines, which can be confusing when it comes to making connections. Second, the maps posted in every Métro car include a stripe for an as yet unfinished fifth line. Only the white dots that are filled in on that map represent currently operative stations. The primary interchanges are the Berri de Montigny and Lionel Groulx stations, from which you can head in any direction.

Taxis are readily available, and can be flagged down at curbside or summoned ahead by your hotel. Fares are $1.20 to start, and 70 cents per kilometer. Tipping is standard procedure—about 15% unless you've gotten extra help with bags or parcels.

The *calèche*, as horse-drawn carriages are known in Montreal, are popular for romantics and families. Most of the drivers are at least moderately well versed in their city's history and sights and will offer appropriate commentary to those who wish. The buggies are lined up at Place Jacques Cartier, down by the waterfront, and at Dominion Square downtown. In winter, the drivers use sleighs instead of carriages, providing blankets for warmth. Bargaining is a way of life for *calèche* rides in summer or winter, though the going rate is approximately $20 for about an hour.

Downtown

Whether it's shopping, discoing, dining, museum and gallery hopping, or just plain strolling, Sherbrooke Street has something for every visitor to Montreal and is an excellent starting point for a day's walking tour of the various downtown districts. From this starting point it is easy to cover the Underground City; the boutiques, *terrasses*, and restaurants of Crescent, Montagne, Bishop, and Mackay; Place Ville Marie; Place Bonaventure; and Place Victoria. It is only a little out of the way to the cultural center Place des Arts, and the spectacular shopping mall Complexe Desjardins.

Sherbrooke is an avenue of class and distinction, not without its haughty overtones, yet, as everywhere in this city, it also represents a coming together of old and new values—whether the Mercantile Bank and Alcan Building, with their original nineteenth-century façades and high-tech towers, or the contrasting versions of "elegance" evinced by the Ritz-Carlton and Le Quatre Saisons (Four Seasons) Hotels. Here, also, are two of Montreal's most impressive museums:

DOWNTOWN 28

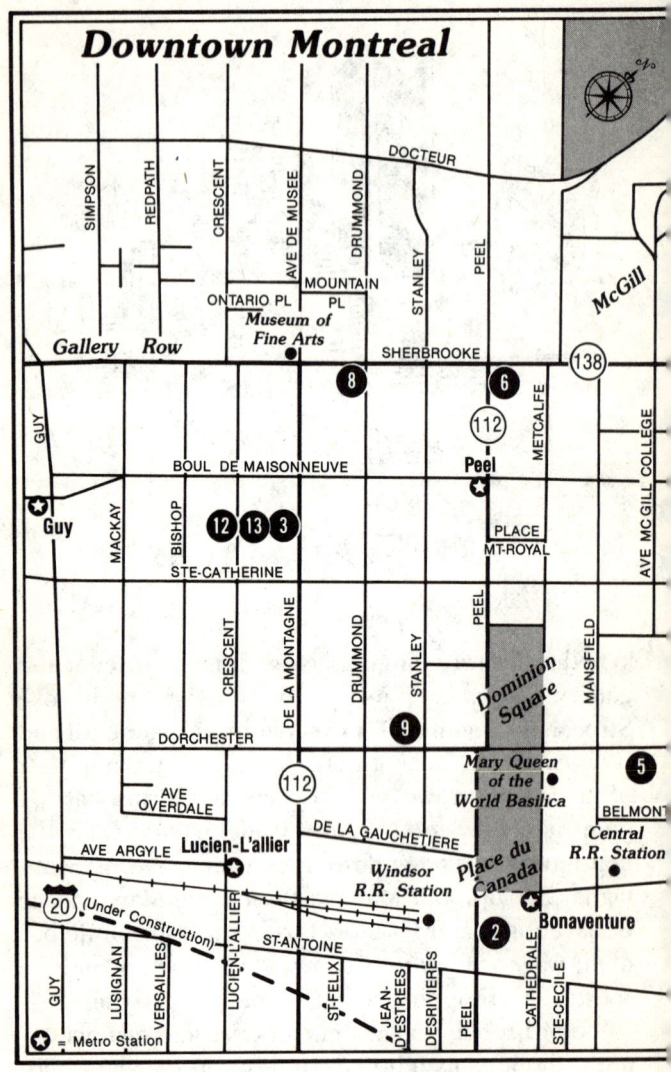

Points of Interest

Hotels
1) Bonaventure Westin
2) Chateau Champlain
3) Hotel de la Montagne
4) Meridien
5) Queen Elizabeth
6) Quatre Saisons
7) Regence Hyatt
8) Ritz Carlton
9) Sheraton Centre

Restaurants
10) Biddles
11) Caveau
12) Les Halles
13) Thursday's

29 DOWNTOWN

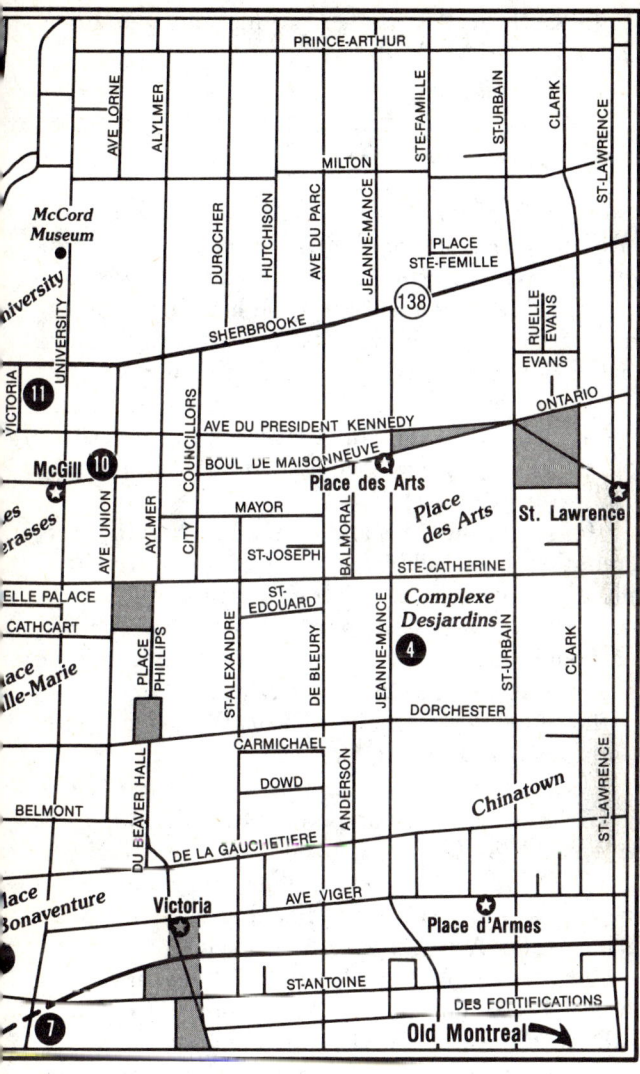

Musée de Beaux Arts (Fine Arts) and the ethnographically oriented McCord.

The **Ritz-Carlton** is a classic old-world hotel, baroque, ornamented, formal and enormously comfortable. With its white-shuttered and canopied outside and glowing gilt lobby it is a sightseeing attraction in itself. Go for tea or breakfast, at least, and sit on the charming outside garden terrace in summer watching the ducks wobble about a small pond. Or stop at the Grand Prix piano bar for a nightcap—a downstairs room that is just dark enough, smokey enough and cozy enough.

Of its various bars and dining rooms, only L'Intercontinentale qualifies as informal. (Men wear dark suits to breakfast in the heat of summer even on the patio.) A $7 business lunch is available, as are similarly reasonably priced *a la carte* entrees midday and for dinner. But there are plenty of better eating options in the immediate vicinity—particularly, for lighter meals, the *terrases* along Crescent Street.

As for the accommodations, this is the place to stay if you want to be pampered to the hilt. A consistent six star (or *fleur-de-lys*) rating means outstandingly comfortable beds, period furniture and a staff that is always ready to serve. When booking, request a room facing Mount Royal—a breathtaking view to catch first thing any morning. With 247 rooms, rates range from about $130–$160 for a double. Parking is extra. As with most Montreal hotels, special packages for tourists, good any day of the week, run about a third less than the regular rate and include such amenities as discount dinner vouchers good at the hotel's restaurants and/or free drinks. Package guests shouldn't expect the best rooms unless business is unusually slow. (1228 Sherbrooke West, corner of Drummond, Montreal H3G 1H6; 514–842–4212.)

Le Quatre Saisons, or the Four Seasons, is even

more expensive: $150–$170 for a double, with packages offered for about $80 per person, double occupancy, for two nights, including a free drink, pastry, and a sightseeing tour (parking extra). Modern simplicity, warm soothing pastels, and central location make Le Quatre Saisons the most inviting of Montreal's top-price, top-service, six *fleur-de-lys* hotels. (The ratings, by the way, are determined by the tourist bureau of Quebec Province; ranging from one to six *fleur-de-lys*, they are generally reliable as a shorthand for cleanliness and comfort.)

The 319 rooms are spacious and comfortable. Buffet luncheon or tea can be taken in the lounge off the main lobby, while drinks are offered in a large sitting area affording a surprising degree of privacy outside meeting and reception rooms on the second floor. If cost is not a factor, a front room, again facing Mount Royal, is the way to go. (1050 Sherbrooke West, near Peel, Montreal H3A 2R6; 514-284-1110).

The dining room Pierre de Coubertin is stiffly formal but top flight. Rhapsodie, a nightclub open Tuesdays through Saturdays from 9:00 P.M. until 3:00 A.M., is something of an adult playroom, complete with pool tables, backgammon, standing bars, couches, and dance floor.

The Museum of Fine Arts, 1379 Sherbrooke West (285-1600), is a few blocks west. The classically styled building, designed by Edward and William Maxwell and opened in 1912, houses a permanent collection including pre-Columbian statues, ancient Oriental ceramics, a good representation of Old European Masters, African masks, Eskimo soapstone sculpture, stained glass, furniture, and more. Its growth prompted the addition of a new wing to the Vermont marble-fronted original under the guidance of architect Fred Lebensold in the mid-1970s.

Major traveling exhibits of photography, painting, and sculpture stop here regularly, with the auditorium used for special art-related film events. If you're planning a stay of some duration, you can even rent artwork by the month through the museum. Closed Mondays; otherwise, the Fine Arts is open 11:00 A.M. to 5:00 P.M., with admission $2 or less. A cafeteria-style coffee shop is available for lunch and snacks, with an outdoor patio open in summer, though better lunch suggestions appear below.

Heading farther west on the opposite side of Sherbrooke, you'll find some of the poshest stores in all of Montreal—so posh, in fact, that you almost never see anybody in some of them. Eighteenth- and nineteenth-century French antiques, Oriental jewelry, and imported clothing from Italy and France are available in these foreboding shops. As for galleries worth visiting:

Eskimo Art, 1434 Sherbrooke West (844–4080) is devoted exclusively (and none too surprisingly) to Eskimo art.

Theo Waddington, 1504 Sherbrooke West (933–3653), is invariably showing the work of the latest post-modern expressionists.

Verre d'Art, 1518 Sherbrooke West (932–3896), has unusual glass art by a variety of Canadian craftspeople.

Elca London, 1616 Sherbrooke West (931–3646), exhibits the paintings, prints, and brass sculpture of up-and-coming contemporary Canadian artists as well as handling an extensive collection of Eskimo soapstone sculpture and art.

In keeping with the gallery spirit, a late luncheon at the Art Deco-influenced Au Papillion Gourmand (the Gourmet Butterfly), 2320 Guy Street (pronounced "Gee" with a hard G), might include artfully conceived fruit, vegetable, or meat-based salad plates that average about $5.50, or sandwiches ranging from $2 to $7. A carafe of wine should accompany all selections, if only to maintain the mood.

DOWNTOWN

Château Versailles, 1659 Sherbrooke West (514-933-3611), back around the corner of Guy, is one of Montreal's most charming and most European-style hotels. Four greystone houses have been connected, creating a total of 70 guest rooms. The basic setting is Victorian, many of the rooms outfitted with genuine antiques—while both modern and period art and sculpture adorn the bright, cheerful hallways and the sitting areas. Nothing elaborate is to be found at the Château Versailles; the rooms are simple, clean, and functional, with full private bath, air conditioning, and TV. There is a breakfast room, and room service offers tea, coffee, hot chocolate, and biscuits between 4:00 P.M. and 11:00 P.M. That's it. No bar, no restaurant.

What the hotel lacks in services it more than compensates for in personalized attention to its guests' needs and comfort. It is doubtful that there is any hotel in Montreal that could be more relaxing. Rates for doubles range from $70–$85, with winter weekend packages considerably less. Reservations are almost always necessary at least a few weeks ahead; unlike most Montreal hotels, Château Versailles has an exceptional occupancy rate that hovers around 85%. Free parking is available, while the Guy Métro stop is two blocks away.

Breakfast or snacks are highly recommended at Boulangerie Au Bon Croissant one block south at the corner of St. Mathieu Street and Lincoln Ave. This is a tiny pastry and gourmet take-out shop with the kitchen right above the store. There are a few stools and a counter inside, and three glass-topped tables outside when weather permits. A breakfast special for $1 brings your choice of coffee including *café au lait*—coffee with steamed milk classically served in a large cereal-bowl—along with a fresh croissant with butter and jam. The fruit tarts, mousses, and Italian pastries are equally interesting breakfast entries. This is also an excellent place to put together a picnic lunch when heading to Mount Royal Park. Pâtés, vegetable salads, cheeses, and bread are all quite good.

The Château Versailles, in fact, is just on the perimeter of Montreal's boutique and singles heartland. To fully appreciate this four-block-by-three-block stretch, count on walking up and down Mackay, Bishop, Crescent, and Montagne, between Sherbrooke and Dorchester, beginning sometime in mid-afternoon if you're serious about shopping (later if not) and timing yourself so as to finish up in time for drinks, dinner, and clubbing at some of the best—and trendiest—spots in town.

Given its position as home to the latest in fads and fashion, this is an area more in a state of flux than transition. Shops come and go, the "hottest" bars and clubs change in a matter of hours (in summer, depending to some extent on where and what time the sun hits the outdoor *terrasses*). You'll discover your own "finds," no doubt, among the boutiques and shops, some of which are described in the shopping section of this book, but the social and culinary scenes seem to have taken somewhat firmer root.

Thursday's, 1449 Crescent (288–5656), is the hub of the action. People seem to be falling out of the place once work is done for the day—huge bar on one floor, restaurant upstairs, and a basement passage to the Victorian-styled Hotel de la Montagne on the backing street. The joke in town is that you can make your pick-up at the bar, dine, go to the basement disco, and inconspicuously escape to the hotel with no problem; there's even a phone in a quiet nook in the passageway so you can call home and say you'll be working late.

If that's the joke, the reality probably isn't far behind. Tiffany lamps, whirring Casablanca ceiling fans, and just enough light and noise to mask any minor personal flaws, set the tone at the bar and at the platformed tables that afford coziness *and* the chance to see and be seen. The restaurant, with everything from salads to *châteaubriand,* is even noisier, with long waits for tables regardless of whether you've made reservations. Expect dinner for two to run $50, though you can easily go higher or lower.

Most people probably don't go for the food in the first place, but if you actually do get a table (and obviously lots of people do), you can sample avacado stuffed with crabmeat, smoked trout with creamed horseradish, eggs Benedict, shrimp Provençal—a basic potpourri of Continental fare. As at many Montreal restaurants, though, beware of items listed on the menu that aren't in season; asparagus is likely to be offered many places no matter the time of year. Can-openers know not the bounds of time.

Hotel de la Montagne, 1430 de la Montagne (between Ste.-Catherine and Maisonneuve) Montreal H3G 1Z5 (514–288–5656), is an unassuming presence on Montagne Street. From the outside it looks like an apartment building (which is what it was prior to becoming a hotel), except for the bellman in uniform. Walking in, you're first struck by the enormous fountain with nude and butterfly in the lobby, and crystal chandelier hanging over a dining area surrounded by oversize plants and statuary. Next you notice the menu displayed at the maître d's desk, the bar, and the tea area. Look about, and the registration desk comes into view off to the left. The rooms maintain the turn-of-the-century flavor and, given its individuality, the hotel's rates are surprisingly within reason: $95 for doubles weekdays and a weekend special for two people, two nights, includes Saturday breakfast and Sunday brunch.

On a summer afternoon or evening, Thursday's and the nearby outdoor cafés Winston Churchill and Tuttles will be filled with patrons, while other bistros and watering holes lie nearly empty. (By the way, glass walls enclose most of these terraces during colder seasons.) Casa Pedro picks up some of the overflow, but as the night wears on, the serious action moves to Bishop, south of Ste.-Catherine Street. This is the area for local young executives and their visiting counterparts, well-heeled and looking to make new friends.

Bishop has a string of American-style bars with names like Woody's and Kazouzz. Woody's is a turn-of-the-century style pub where they wait in line to get a place at the bar, with the steps leading in as crowded as the room proper. All serve hamburgers, salads, and quiche—typical inexpensive bar food that goes well with Molson's or other Canadian beer. Le Club Mingus Miles, and Le Club Faces a bit farther down the block, have jazz and rock. Among the more exclusive discos—a basement room behind imposing closed black doors—is P.K.'s.

This is also one of Montreal's primary restaurant districts. Do keep in mind that even the most expensive restaurants here and all over the city have special "businessmen's" lunches—three courses that are almost always in the $6–$8 per person range. They aren't quite as extravagant as regularly priced offerings, and they are not available weekends or holidays, but they come from the same kitchens and are generally up to the standards upon which the restaurants' reputations are based. As a way of sampling the best Montreal has to offer at very, very reasonable prices, they can't be beat.

Les Halles, 1450 Crescent, between Maisonneuve and Ste.-Catherine (844–2328), and its sister La Petite Halle, 1425 Bishop, between Ste.-Catherine and Dorchester (849–1294), are justifiably among Montreal's best-known dining establishments. The former is the more formal and gastronomically imposing, despite the lighthearted country-market murals that adorn the walls and the equal welcome given both to those who look as though they've just stepped out of a fashion magazine and to those who've been sightseeing in casual clothes all day. Dining rooms on two floors of a greystone house, however, serve up an impressive cross between classic French and nouvelle cuisines.

On the parlor floor, a *charcuterie* counter at the rear turns out freshly sliced salmon, homemade sausages, and a variety of pâtés and terrines. One item not included on the menu but typical of some of the more interesting fare features chunks of lobster housed in salmon mousse and bound by paper-thin smoked salmon—the entire concoction topped, no less, with truffles. Another appetizer that *is* listed offers sliced breast of duck with black currant sauce.

Typical entrées include steaks in a variety of sauces, veal in a basil sauce, and poached, sautéed, grilled, and otherwise none-too-simply prepared fish and seafood. Desserts range from standard tortes and mousses to exotic fruit creations such as raspberry mousse cake with whole raspberries drenched in a spiked raspberry purée and decorated with poached figs and fresh mango—as much a sight to behold as it is delectable.

There are two drawbacks to dining at Les Halles: First, the check for three courses will easily top $100 for two people imbibing a moderately priced bottle of wine and including tip (though in terms of value for the money it is still outstanding, if hardly a bargain. Reminder: the "businessmen's lunch" *is* a bargain). The second drawback is that you need patience; the kitchen is small and cannot handle the number of patrons it feeds. Waits between appetizers and main courses can run in excess of an hour.

La Petite Halle is equally cheerful in its French country charm and just as creative in its kitchen, albeit in a more limited and less costly way. One menu is served throughout the day from 11:45 A.M. until 10:30 P.M. weekdays, as well as for Sunday brunch (perhaps the best time to go, as it is least crowded then) beginning at noon. Soups, salads, *cassoulet*, omelets ($2.20 to $7), crêpes, quiches, sauerkraut, steaks . . . something for every palate and budget. As do many restaurants in Montreal, La Petite Halle closes for the month of July.

Les Chenets, 2075 Bishop (844–1842), located in adjoining stone houses, is known to many Montrealers as their city's most expensive restaurant. A $125 special dinner for two, including two half-bottles of wine, offers turbot as its fish dish, beef Wellington for meat and a Cointreau soufflé for dessert. With indulgence its *raison d'être,* this is not a place to go if you're counting either pennies or calories. Seasonal *à la carte* offerings might include tripe at $14.50 and lobster thermidor for $22; a typically excellent fixed-price lunch, at $6.50 for three courses, might combine cucumber salad, rabbit, and dessert. Entrées at lunch run $4.50 to $12.50 *à la carte.*

Also worth investigating in this area:

Le Mas des Olivier, 1216 Bishop (861–6733). Provençal dishes such as breast of duck in green peppercorn sauce, trout braised with fennel, and sweetbreads in port are part of full dinners priced from $13–$17.

Elysée Mandarin, 1221 Mackay (866–5975). A Montreal transplant of a Parisian Chinese restaurant specializing in food of the Peking and Szechuan provinces. Full dinners and sharing keep the prices to within $15 a person.

Le Tricolore, 2065 Bishop (843–7745), has a seven-course *menu degustation* at $37.50 and complete three-course business lunches for $5–$7.50.

La Maison Coreenne, 1219 Mackay (861–6128), where Korean-style hibachis are placed at your table for barbequing fish, seafood, and meats.

The tour of downtown continues eastward again at Sherbrooke, where you enter the hypothetical boundaries of Montreal's Golden Square Mile—once the stomping ground of the city's wealthiest dwellers. During the nineteenth century this area was dominated by country-style estates; up until the 1950s it also enjoyed a reputation as home to many international embassies. A handful of consulates and many of the homes remain, though almost all can be viewed by the general public from the outside only.

To the left (north) at Museum Avenue you pass a row of old coach houses; to the right at Drummond is the Italian Renaissance-styled Mount Stephen Club; on Sherbrooke itself are such outstanding monuments to late nineteenth-century masonry as Corby House. On Sherbrooke between Drummond and Stanley is the gleaming new Maison Alcan, an office building with boutiques and restaurants on the ground level. Le Pavillon d'Atlantique is one of Montreal's best known (and most expensive) seafood houses newly ensconced in these most spectacular surroundings. Also of note is La Tulipe Noire (285–1225), serving hot meals but favored for its chocolates and pastries. La Tulipe Noire is open until midnight most evenings. Stanley Street is a throwback to Victorian times while the recently renamed Docteur Penfield Avenue (still referred to on many maps by its original name, McGregor Avenue) has the few remaining mansions from the estates of yore. The architecturally minded can find detailed descriptions of these homes—and those that have been demolished in the name of progress—in *Montreal Guide* (Libre Expression, $14.95, available at most Canadian book shops).

Hotel Le Merlion, 1240 Drummond, Montreal H3G 1V7 (514-866-6492), a half block from Ste. Catherine St., is convenient, unassuming, and very moderately priced. Doubles run about $45–$55, and parking is inexpensively available. It is particularly popular among business people who aren't concerned with luxury.

The McCord Museum, 690 Sherbrooke West (392-4778), houses an outstanding ethnography collection that features everything from Victorian dresses to contemporary Canadian photography to Eskimo totem poles. One prominent example of the latter dominates the building's interior; the central staircase winds around it, affording views from different vantage points. The present home for the McCord was opened in 1971, more than fifty years after its original benefactor, David Ross McCord, donated his personal collection of Canadiana to McGill University. The McCord is open Wednesday through Sunday 11:00 A.M. to 5:00 P.M.; admission is $2 or less.

Across Sherbrooke at McGill Street is the entrance to the English-language McGill University campus. A striking mix of old and new buildings, its medical and engineering facilities stick out like sore thumbs—especially when viewed from Mount Royal. Particularly worth noting is Durocher Street, the oldest street in the district, dating to the early 1800s. The campus is open to strollers for a pleasant if unspectacular detour.

McGill's 1,000 **student apartments** are open to students during the summer for the very reasonable rate of $22 per day single, $34 double. The location and setting couldn't be better, and you even have the option of preparing your own morning coffee; given that these are apartments rather than dorms, each has full kitchen facilities. Glamour, no; cost effective and functional, yes. While rooms are usually available, reservations are always advisable. Residences des etudiants de l'universite McGill, 3935 University, Montreal H3A 2B4; 514-392-4224.

With a large student population right at hand, you'd almost expect to find a great jazz club in the vicinity, and you do, with Biddles, 2060 Aylmer St. (842-8656). Owner Charles Biddle, a professorial-looking jazz bassist with gray hair and beard and usually wearing a dark three-piece suit, is on the stage when he isn't playing the lounge at the Queen Elizabeth Hotel or touring Canada. The room is multi-tiered, giving a good view of the tiny stage tucked in the corner. Violins and cornets hang from the ceiling, there are etched glass and art-deco light columns behind the bar, a moose head, stained glass lamps, etc. Biddle happily eyes the crowd from the stage as waiters and waitresses bring barbequed ribs and chicken to patrons. Drinks are about $4, but there's no minimum unless there's a big name joining Biddle on the bandstand—as the likes of Sarah Vaughan have been wont to do.

Heading south on University Street brings you to downtown's shopping mecca. Eaton's, The Bay, Ogilvy's, and Simpson's are the main department stores, all located off Ste. Catherine Street—itself the main street-level shopping avenue in Montreal. Another block south is Place Ville Marie, the hub of Montreal's Underground City and home to the main, year-round Tourist Information Office.

Capping this plaza is the startling 45-floor cruciform skyscraper (also referred to as Place Ville Marie) designed by I.M. Pei for the Royal Bank. Below are dozens of shops constituting one of the most interesting legs of Montreal's Underground City, bested, perhaps, only by the multi-tiered and architecturally more interesting Complexe Desjardins opposite Place des Arts (and incorporating the Meridien Hotel). More on the latter shortly. At Place Ville Marie, designer names abound, as do book, linen, record, toy, fast-food, and other specialty stores.

A note here about the Underground City. There are six major branches to it, all connected via Métro stops so you need never face inclement weather. Latest available statistics claim that 1,015 boutiques, 128 restaurants, 22 movie houses, four theaters, eight hotels, and 25 bank branches are linked through the network. By far the most interesting concentrations of stores and restaurants are those beneath Place Ville Marie and Place Bonaventure (which are connected), and at Complexe Desjardins (adjacent to Place des Arts). "The City Below," a leaflet available from the

Tourist Information Office, maps out the Underground City complete with its Métro stops.

At the other extreme, atop the Place Ville Marie is Altitude 737, a restaurant named for its location. A luncheon buffet at $16.50 and *table d'hôte* dinners at $25 are offered. *A la carte* service is also available, and a bar is open from noon until well after midnight. The latter is a good place to rest weary feet and enjoy the view; for the money you'll do better dining elsewhere; Altitude 727 is the neighboring disco.

Hotel La Reine Elizabeth, 900 Dorchester West, Montreal H3B 4A5 (514–861–3511), is across from Place Ville Marie. Because of its location, size (more than 1,100 rooms), and its function as central depot for bus and rail passengers, the Queen Elizabeth is exceedingly popular. A stroll through the lobby, however, is akin to walking through a bus station. Tour groups and local conventions are the hotel's mainstays, and while half-price tourist packages can make this a reasonable place for bedding down, it is not a hotel offering much in the way of personalized service. Doubles run about $110–$150; parking is extra.

The Beaver Club, the hotel's most famous dining room, is an anachronism: Located practically in the lobby of this bustling tourist lodge, the dining hall itself is as clubby as the hunting image its name suggests. Even its insignia carries the old-fashioned image. Yet the kitchen is known near and far as a purveyor of the latest in nouvelle cuisine. The regular *table d'hôte* menu doesn't reflect it, with its roast rib of western beef *au jus* served with baked potato, broiled tomato and tossed salad ($23.75), or sweet and sour chicken, glazed carrots, and tiny peas ($20.50). Daily specials include duck with a purée of leeks and turnips, gently sauced fresh fish, and delectably light pastries. The clubhouse atmosphere is overwhelming, though. Jacket and tie for men are also a must.

Bonaventure Hilton International, 1 Place Bonaventure, Montreal H5A 1E4 (514–878–2332), is a much more inviting hotel just a few blocks away. Set atop an office building whose main entrance leads to another leg of the Underground City. There is an elevator to the lobby. Despite almost 400 rooms, the ambience is that of a small, cozy hotel, though long checkout lines are likely to send you off on a bad note. Off the lobby are a garden to one side and, on the other, an outdoor pool that is open all year round. The rooms are in split-level wings—modern, clean, and all overlooking the city. Regular rates are high—$140–$155 for a double, with parking extra, but discounts are often available.

Regence Hyatt, 777 University, Montreal H3C 3Z7 (514–879–1370), a bit to the southwest at Place Victoria and bordering on Old Montreal, is slightly out of the mainstream and thus relatively inexpensive $100–$110 for doubles, with package deals available. It is a large, bustling (even when there are few people around) hotel, best-suited to conventioneers or those who want to be in walking distance of the old city. Impossible to miss at nearby Place Victoria is the 47-floor Stock Exchange Tower—*the* symbol of Montreal's new financial district.

Going west again on Dorchester you will pass Mary Queen of the World Cathedral, constructed between 1875 and 1894 as a copy of St. Peter's in Rome. The row of statues atop the Greek columns is beautifully illuminated at night. At the next corner is Dominion Square. Bus tours and horse drawn *calèche* rides depart from here; in summer there is a shack housing a second branch of the Convention and Visitor's Bureau. On the square is also the former Hotel Windsor —at one time Montreal's grandest hostelry.

The Montreal Planetarium, 1000 Saint-Jacques St. (872–4210), is a few blocks south on Peel Street. Programs change every eight to ten weeks, but always combine the feats of the impressive Zeiss star projector (illuminating the planets in a field of 9,000 stars) and more than 200 special-effects generators. The one-hour shows can simulate the sky as it would be seen by the naked eye at any given time over a 25,000-year period. A small admission fee is charged.

Le Chateau Champlain, 1050 de la Gauchetiere West, Montreal H3B 4C9 (514–878–1688), is a few blocks' walk south on Peel St. It is modern and warm, with a small maze of shops, dining facilities, and a movie theater. The way the lobby is laid out you would hardly know the hotel services 600 rooms ($125–$150 for doubles, parking extra). Le Caf' Conc', with its Moulin Rouge-type show complete with Can Can girls, is one of the more popular supper clubs.

Le Centre Sheraton, 1201 Dorchester West (near Peel), Montreal H3B 2L7 (514–878–2000), is another hotel best made for large groups, though its public sitting and drinking areas give it a certain degree of coziness while pool, sauna and gym facilities are excellent. Convenient to both the Dominion Square/Place Ville Marie and Crescent/Bishop areas. Doubles go for $90–$130, parking extra, and there's a rooftop restaurant with more great views of the city.

Place des Arts, toward the eastern end of Ste. Catherine Street, houses the Salle Wilfrid-Pelletier for opera, symphonies, and ballet, and the Theatre Maisonneuve and Theatre Port-Royal for additional stage presentations. Boldly modern and decorated with much Canadian art—eight ceramic friezes by Jordi Bonet are especially impressive in Salle Wilfrid-Pelletier—the three houses entertain nearly 1.5 million people annually with some 900 performances. In addition to regular Montreal Symphony Orchestra concerts, other resident companies include L'Opéra de Montreal and Les grand Ballets Canadiens. There are free lunchtime concerts during the winter in the second floor foyer of Salle Wilfrid-Pelletier. Unfortunately, there are almost no performances here during the summer.

Underground corridors connect Place des Arts with the Métro, Complexe Desjardins, and the Hotel Meridien. Complexe Desjardins is physically the most spectacular of Montreal's indoor shopping centers, with large wood sculptures and mobiles in an immense atrium. The stores are on tiers that circle that atrium, with TV shows broadcast from a little stage. Window shopping is possible here 24 hours a day. The rest of the neighborhood outside along Sherbrooke is—surprisingly—home to X-rated movie houses and junky souvenir shops.

Hotel Meridien, 4 Complexe Desjardins, Montreal H5B 1E5 (514–285–1450), is perfect for those whose focus is the performing arts, though it is a little removed from other main attractions. Colorfully modern, it's a busy hotel with more than 600 rooms (doubles $100–$120), popular among business travelers and sophisticated young couples who take advantage of special tourist rates.

Chinatown is a nearby favorite for inexpensive dining. Though it is only a few blocks long on Lagauchetiere between St. Denis and St. Lawrence Blvd., there are several dozen colorful restaurants and shops maintained by the 300 or so Orientals who reside in the area. The district is increasingly hemmed in by construction all around it; how well it will be able to stand up to the bulldozers that appear to be closing in on it remains to be seen.

There are a number of plain, clean, and well-run medium-priced hotels in the downtown area. The tourist packages available at some of the best hotels come out less expensive than the regular rates at some of these establishments. You may, however, want to check for possible special rates at these as well. Among the possibilities:

Le Sherbourg, 475 Sherbrooke West, Montreal H3A 2L9 (514–842–3961), centrally located and popular with bus tour groups. Doubles range from $80–$95.

Quality Inn centre-ville, 410 Sherbrooke West, Montreal H3A 1B3 (514–844–8851), offers the same front-room views of Mount Royal as its relatively nearby neighbors the Ritz and the Four Seasons—only at $75–$85 for a double.

Holiday Inn centre-ville, 420 Sherbrooke West, Montreal H3A 14B (514–842–6111), is similar to the Quality Inn, though the latter is somewhat newer. Prices are also roughly similar.

Royal Roussillon, 1610 Saint-Hubert, Montreal H2L 3Z3 (514–849–3214), is next door to the main bus terminal, which has its good and bad points. Again, a four *fleur-de-lys* rating from the province seems high, but relative to the $30–$50 room rate for doubles, the proportions just may work out.

A number of other sights and neighborhoods within easy reach of the central downtown area are worth consideration:

St. Joseph's Oratory and Montreal University. The No. 115 bus heading north at the corner of Sherbrooke and Guy will route you by the Canadian Jewish Congress building, along the outskirts of Westmount (historically an Anglo-Saxon region, though changing rapidly), past Mount Royal Park and into the Côte des Neiges district. St. Joseph's Oratory is accessible from Queen Mary Road. Started in 1904 with a simple wooden chapel that still stands, the shrine today is dominated by the domed basilica that reaches 856 feet (261 meters) into the sky. Though its interior is hardly as interesting as the outside or the grounds around the Oratory, its history as a church of healing (through prayer to St. Joseph) draws some two million pilgrims to the site annually.

As you leave St. Joseph's, continue north on Côte des Neiges, turning right (west) at Edouard-Montpetit Blvd. The French-speaking Montreal University is here, open to walkers, though its modern structures may not seem as inviting as McGill's. Like McGill, the University opens its **student apartments** to tourists (students and non-students) in the summer. Single rooms only are available at about $20, less for students; weekly rates are also available. (Residences des etudiants de l'universite de Montreal, 2350 Edouard-Montpetit, Montreal H3C 1J4, 514-343-6531.)

Parc Avenue, which runs just east of Mount Royal Park, is a fascinating tour through a series of neighborhoods that changes dramatically every few blocks.

Begin with breakfast or brunch at **Beauty's**, 93 Mount Royal Ave. West (849-8883), about five blocks from the Mont Royal Métro station and one block east of Parc. Beauty's has been gussied up with something between Art Deco and high-tech trappings since its humble luncheonette origins, but the Beauty's Special and Mish-Mash are as they have always been since 1942: the former a toasted, sesame seed-coated bagel piled high with cream cheese, smoked salmon (*a.k.a.* lox), Bermuda onion, and tomato. The latter is an omelette filled with frankfurters, salami, green pepper, and fried onions, among other things.

Orange juice is freshly squeezed and served in large glasses—$1.25 for the "regular" and $1.75 for the giant. It's breakfast all day, here, despite other kinds of entrées being available. We saw someone ask for a slice of carrot cake topped with yogurt and fresh fruit, and darned if the somewhat surprised waitress didn't put together a towering (and highly attractive) plate. Friendly is the word—so much so that the lines on weekend mornings are long. Seats at the stainless steel counter can be had the quickest, but a visit is definitely a must. (No wait weekdays.)

Parc Avenue itself is a study in change. For the most part, the ethnic restaurants and shops located here are plain, "unprettified," and inexpensive. The Greek district, for example, is quite unlike what is now found on Prince Arthur Street—where moussaka has become trendy. Yet there are signs that gentrification is afoot here, too. A beautiful Art-Deco bistro, seems oddly out of place at first, but other similarly modish shops and bars pop up on the side streets and along Parc even in the most working class sections—which not coincidentally border on the upscale neighborhood of Outremont.

L'Odéon, 4806 Parc Ave. (273–4088), is the aforementioned Art Deco, albeit cum high tech, bistro. That's probably enough to suggest it's a noisy, friendly and fashionable place where a tantalizingly arranged pot au feu, an unlikely but immensely enjoyable chicken with melon balls and a simple cold roast beef with mustard sauce are among featured selections in summer. Desserts sit temptingly at the center of the room—try the excellent lemon mousse or any of a number of chocolate confections. Dinner for two will run $70 with wine and tip.

Laurier Street, which runs perpendicular to Parc, is Outremont's classy shopping block. Antique stores, boutiques, and a handful of coffee shops and restaurants that are pricey and exclusive and entirely different in tone from that of its immediate surroundings.

Cafe Laurier, 394 Laurier West (273–2484), is *the* meeting place in the area—whether shoppers at midday or singles into the wee hours, with a menu that caters to all possible appetites. The biggest plus: it's open until 3 A.M. weekends, 2 A.M. other days.

Finish off this tour with a visit to the Fairmount Montreal Bagel Bakery, 263 St. Viateur. You can watch the bakers roll their bagels seven days a week. Don't be surprised by the lines Saturday night; and/or at **Symposium Des Dieux Restaurant,** 5334 Parc (274-9547). Symposium is a two-floor Greek restaurant serving only fish and seafood downstairs. The waiter brings over a tray with the day's catch, allowing you to choose your dinner. Upstairs, there is bouzouki music and bellydancing every night except Mondays, along with a more balanced menu of meats and fish. A full meal will not likely run to as much as $10 a person. (Don't confuse this establishment with Symposium on St. Denis; the latter is neither as good nor as inexpensive as the one described here.)

Additional sights within easy reach of downtown:

Montreal's zoo has both summer and winter homes on the outskirts of downtown. La Fontaine Park's four-acre Garden of Wonders is a summertime petting zoo built around nursery rhyme themes. A short walk from the Sherbrooke Métro station along Cherrier Street takes you right into the park. There are daily porpoise shows, and while the zoo is definitely geared to young children, its setting in the heart of the park makes it a good stop as part of a picnic. Hours are 10:00 A.M. to sundown, May to September.

At the Winter Zoo, in Angrignon Park in southwest Montreal (Angrignon Métro stop), most of the animals are housed in stone or glass houses, while the llamas and deer are kept in outdoor pens. The zoo is open from noon to 6:00 P.M. Saturdays, Sundays, and holidays, from October through April; from mid-December through Mardi Gras it is open daily from 10:00 A.M. to 10:00 P.M. A small admission fee—$2 or less—is charged.

Château Dufresne, Sherbrooke East and Pie IX Blvd. (514-259-2575), is a turn-of-the-century home that is now a museum of decorative arts.

Old Montreal

The narrow, winding, sometimes cobblestoned streets of Le Vieux Montréal, or the old city of Montreal, exude a sense of history, of conflicting artistic sensibilities, of revitalization that is at once miraculous and painstaking. Leave plenty of time for walking here, for looking up at some of Montreal's most impressive eighteenth- and nineteenth-century architecture. Plan to eat here—at any of several fine bistros or top haute and nouvelle cuisine restaurants.

This will be an area for window shopping (and buying) if your interest is in crafts or furniture. There are *calèche* rides, river cruises (in summer), a flea market on Sundays. Cafés are everywhere, with bountiful outdoor *terrasses* when the weather allows. Check for symphony concerts and organ recitals at Notre Dame, or for hot jazz at L'Air Du Temps. As everywhere in Montreal, the old and the new coexist in sometimes surprising harmony, even in Le Vieux Montréal!

OLD MONTREAL

Old Montreal is most conveniently reached via the Champs de Mars Métro station. Champs de Mars is itself a miniature museum of glass and light. 2,000 square feet of brilliantly colored stained glass designed by Marcelle Ferron house the above-ground entrance. A quick look to the left as you exit the station finds the castle-like former Viger Hotel towering above. Though used as a municipal building for more than 30 years, it still bespeaks the elegance of an era long gone by.

Continue straight, making a right onto Notre Dame Street. Pass City Hall (Hotel de Ville) on the right and Château Ramezay on the left—more about both in a moment—and head straight to Place Jacques Cartier, which begins at the head of St. Paul Street. Cartier was the first European to land on the island of Montreal, in 1535, proclaiming it *"un mont réal"* in honor of the mountain that stands at its center. Today he is honored by the square before you that overlooks the harbor on the St. Lawrence Seaway.

During peak tourist periods in the summer the square becomes a pedestrian mall that is closed to motorized traffic. Flower and fruit stands and street performers populate the center of the square, while cafés and restaurants line its outer edges. St. Amable Street is a small alleyway, right off the plaza, that is lined by artists and jewelry makers in summer. Restoration of these buildings, many of which date back to the eighteenth century, has been (and continues to be) an on-going process. Former hotels are now condominium apartments, while restaurants such as the famed La Marée and Le St. Amable, housed in early nineteenth-century private homes, retain the ambience of formal luxury in small, beautifully appointed dining rooms. For all the renovation, it is easy to forget that this is North America at all; this could be a harbor village in France—in another century.

OLD MONTREAL 52

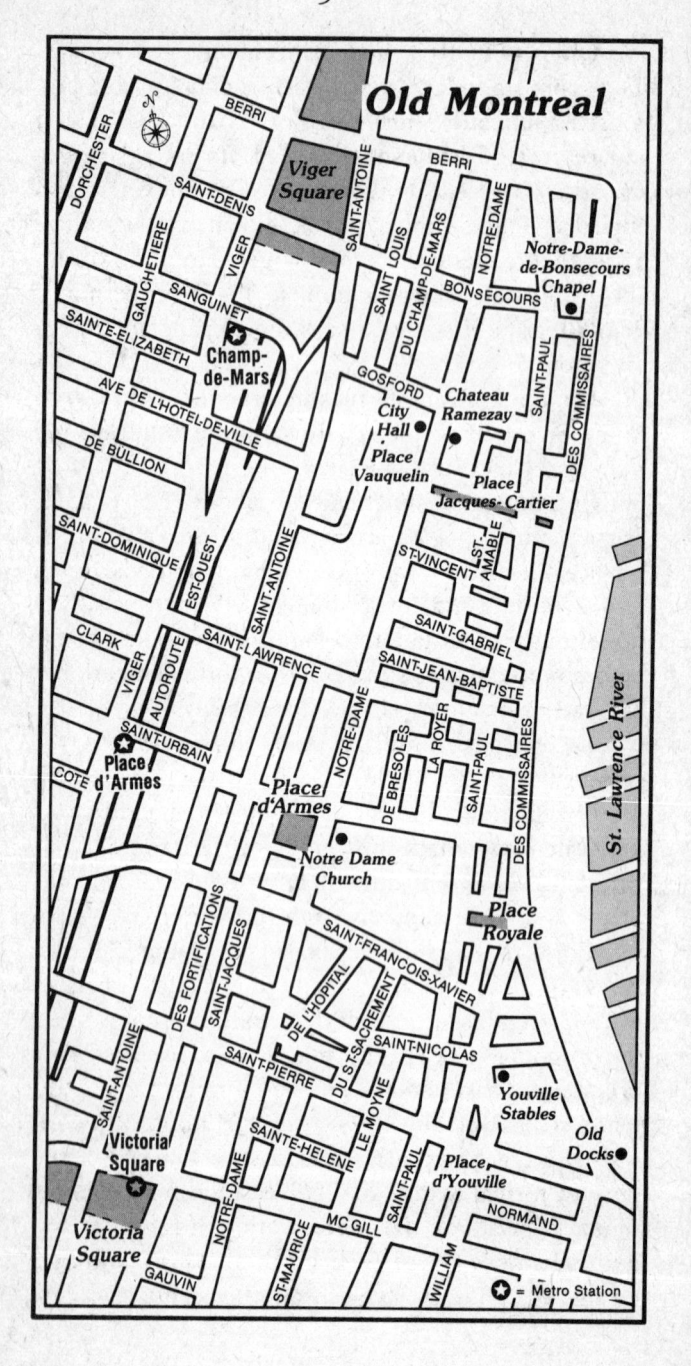

La Marée, 404 Place Jacques Cartier (861–9794), is an absolutely first-rate classical French restaurant. Walk in and you are greeted by a buffet of pâtés, terrines, fresh fish and meats, and pastries—enough to indicate that choosing from the extensive menu is going to be difficult. The maitre d'hôte will be helpful, though, inquiring as to general preferences and then suggesting the day's specialties accordingly. A trout stuffed with a mousse of lobster and fresh vegetables, then braised in Champagne; rack of lamb with herbs and hazelnut butter; veal in a Cognac and Grand Marnier sauce. Cream sauces abound, as do truffles. The soups are thick and rich, perfect for coming in from the cold in winter. The desserts appear delicate, but are no less hearty.

Almost everything seems to be prepared at your table in gleaming copper pans, dished out onto carefully arranged plates by waiters whose attentiveness borders on the obsessive. We once witnessed a virtuosic performance built around the creation of crêpes Marée—the restaurant's own variation on crêpes Suzette—with the waiter squeezing citrus fruits around a fork, running to the kitchen for a bowl of sugar, sprinkling a tiny amount into his mixture, running to return the sugar bowl, and serving the flaming dish to his patrons! It was a 35-minute show with no extra charge for theatrics.

Dinner at La Marée is an event to be savored over hours, with fine wine and as much of an eye toward the staging as a palate for tasting. It is a softly lit restaurant with fresh flowers all around, and you sit in wonderfully comfortable overstuffed chairs at tables that allow for intimacy as well as a few stolen glances to see what those nearby are eating. Inexpensive "business lunches" are available for $6–$10; expect dinner for two to near $100 with a moderately priced bottle of wine.

Le St. Amable, 188 St.-Amable Street (866–

3471), is right next door to La Marée, its entrance on the small sidestreet that is likely to have artists and crafts people hawking their latest creations. Inside is another classic French kitchen and dining room—favored by some Montrealers over La Marée's. Start with a small crêpe filled with crab meat and accompanied by mussels and a lobster sauce or a casserole of snails in a cream sauce with shallots, egg, and Champagne cognac and work your way through to soufflés prepared to your wishes and doused generously with liqueurs. Sample special lunches Monday through Friday from $5–$8 or dine lavishly in the evening for about $80 for two.

The remaining restaurants along Place Jacques Cartier are more average in both price and quality. Any will do fine for a drink or coffee and observing the street scene. Other establishments for less grandiose dining (and some in league with La Marée and Le St. Amable) will be found on the many sidestreets in the old city and discussed throughout this section.

The harbor area itself, at the foot of Place Jacques Cartier, is being developed into an elaborate public site for cafés, exhibits, and live performances. Anchored at the main pier on St. Paul Street are several barges for drinking and sunning, one topped with sand to resemble a beach.

While the surrounding view of dilapidated docks is not especially inviting, the festival atmosphere created by clowns, jugglers, magicians, singers, balloon sculptors, concerts, folk dancing, cotton candy, ice cream, tours of 19th-century tall ships and so on during the summer months is helping rehabilitate the waterfront. Much of the activity is overly commercialized, but such revitalization must be funded somehow. The $3–$4 ticket price allows visitors to leave the pier and return as often as they wish during any one day and includes admission to most of the live performances. A flea market is also open on Sundays during the summer months.

Having explored Place Jacques Cartier and established bearings within the old city, begin your walking tour at City Hall. If you happen to be in Montreal on a Wednesday, check with the Museum of Fine Arts or the Tourist Bureau (the latter has an office on the southwest corner of Notre Dame and Place Jacques Cartier) for free walking tours conducted by volunteers trained by the Museum. The tours are available in English or French and provide an outstanding quick (hour and a half) introduction to the area. The well-versed guides offer just enough social and architectural history for the average tourist, but do not enter any buildings. Groups of about fifteen people each depart from the fountain in the plaza just west of City Hall—Place Vauquelin—beginning promptly at 11:00 A.M. Across Notre Dame and at the top of Place Jacques Cartier is Nelson's Column, a monument to Lord Horatio Nelson, who defeated Napolean. The current statue is a replica of the original erected in 1809.

City Hall was first constructed in 1878 and rebuilt following a fire in the 1920s. It is from the top of this building's steps that the late French President Charles de Gaulle made his infamous speech calling for a "free" Quebec. The building's spectacular marble foyer, with stunning standing Art-Deco lamps, was opened to the public for the first time in the summer of 1983 for an exhibition of paintings of Montreal. The interior is indeed impressive and worth a stop regardless of the current exhibition.

Directly across the street from City Hall is Château Ramezay, built in 1705 and named for its first resident, the eleventh governor of Montreal, Claude de Ramezay. A museum devoted to furniture, clothing, and art of the eighteenth century, its rubble stone exterior with cut stone trim around the windows and dormer windows on top is typical of buildings from that era. The S-hooks on its outer wall are iron bars that extend through the house's interior beams, while a high side wall on the outside serves as a fire wall to protect the edifice from those neighboring it. Château Ramezay is open 10:00 A.M. to 4:30 P.M., Tuesdays through Sundays (861-7182); there is a nominal admission charge.

Continue east on Notre Dame, turning right onto Bonsecours Street. At the foot of the block is Notre-Dame-de-Bonsecours. Begun in 1657, the original wood chapel was completed in 1675 and reconstructed, with additional wings added over the years ever since. Favored by sailors who come to the church to give thanks for safe voyages, the original statue of Virgin Mary brought from France in 1672 for this chapel was miraculously unharmed in a 1754 fire. It is housed now at Maison Mère de la Congregation Notre Dame on Sherbrooke, while a replica stands in its place over the entrance. The interior is very ostentatious (which somehow makes the neon sign facing the harbor seem less out of place) and includes a small museum about the life of Marguerite Bourgeoys, who first conceived the idea for the chapel. There is also a bell tower that can be climbed.

Maison Papineau, 440 Bonsecours, is an unspectacular-looking house built in 1692 of four-foot-thick walls. It is notable because it was purchased by local music critic Eric McLean and restored in the early 1960s. McLean's efforts paved the way for others to seek out, rebuild, and move into similar old homes—and blossomed into the revitalization of the entire Old Montreal area.

Maison du Calvet, 401 Bonsecours, was built some 80 years after Maison Papineau and restored by the Ogilvy department store upon the latter's 100th anniversary. It was closed to the public as of this writing, with no indication of when it would reopen. It houses a museum of early Quebec furniture.

Les Filles du Roy, 415 Bonsecours Street (849-3535), is a festive, bustling restaurant in an old fieldstone-walled house where the waitresses wear native Quebec costumes. There are several dining rooms, the nicest down a short flight of steps from the bar and reception area—darkly medieval but strangely welcoming. The bar itself is skylit, with a terrace out back (not always open) and white wicker furniture inside. Quebec-style food, hearty fare for laborers, is served: heavy on pork and other meats and generously sweetened desserts. Les Filles du Roy is rightly popular among tourists and families, for you get a taste of a local cuisine and color even if the food itself is only moderately enticing. Lunches from $4–$9, with *à la carte* main dishes at dinner from $6.50–$20.

Continue westward at St. Paul Street past the block-long market building on the left. First built in 1845 and topped some twenty years later with a renaissance-style dome, the building has served at various times as a market, a city hall, and a temporary Parliament; it has also suffered numerous fires, the latest in 1979. Restored once again, it houses municipal offices today.

Rasco's Hotel, 295 St. Paul Street, also now occupied by city offices, was once noted as one of Canada's finest hotels, with concert hall, ballroom, and luxurious restaurant. Constructed in 1836, its restoration has sadly done nothing to retain its original architectural splendor.

Le Fadeau, 423 St.-Claude Street (878-3959), doesn't make as much of a show out of dinner as La Marée or Le St. Amable, but the cuisine is of the lighter *nouvelle* orientation and the service a little less intrusive. A *menu degustation* of eight courses for about $40 per person is available, provided everyone at the table has the same. No advance notice is needed unless you plan to dine especially late in the evening. Chef Henri Wojcik instituted the concept of such meals to Montreal, the idea being to enable patrons to sample modest portions of a wide variety of specially prepared dishes. *Table d'hôte* lunches run about $10, while *à la carte* appetizers and desserts at dinner are sufficiently ample to warrant sharing—which could contain the cost of a first-class meal to $60 for two.

L'Empreinte, 272 St. Paul Street East, is an artists' cooperative with very original leather, weaving, batik, pottery, and clothing for sale. Very few artists are represented, but those who are are genuine craftsmakers in a class far above most of the crafts shops you'll encounter farther along on St. Paul. These others (Le Rouet at No. 136 West or Maison Saint Paul at No. 140 West) feature work by Canadian artists but the merchandise is standard tourist-shop fare in quantities that make it difficult to believe each piece is hand-crafted. At L'Empreinte, on the other hand, you may find two-of-a-kind, but it's doubtful unless you are talking about a matched pair of earrings. Le Coq D'Argent, 155 St. Paul East, has Innuit silver jewelry and wood carvings.

Cafés, a variety of ethnic restaurants—Menard at 256 St. Paul East features a Moroccan floor show complete with belly dancers and singers—and several fast-food and take-out places line the street as you reapproach Place Jacques Cartier. St. Paul on the west side of the plaza boasts numerous boutiques, restaurants, discos, and bars. Worth noting:

La Maison Casavant, 206 St. Paul West, for reproductions of French country furniture.

L'Air du Temps, 191 St. Paul West, probably the finest club in the city for latter-day jazz. Tables are practically *on* the tiny bandstand; admission is $3–$5 Thursdays, Fridays, and Saturdays, free other nights; drinks are reasonable. The only caveat: no air conditioning in summer and no cross-ventilation, either. There are early evening sets—usually piano music—

followed by the featured performer going on around 9:30 P.M.

MQ Antiques, 180 St. Paul West, with furniture "inspired by" 19th-century designers and heavy on pine and brass.

Le Muscadin, 100 St. Paul West (842–0588). Italian food is served here in a brick-and-barnwood setting with highly polished wood tables and club chairs. A strange array of barn implements and kitchen utensils adorn the walls, but the fresh, heavily buttered garlic bread with thin slices of tomato that arrives shortly after you've ordered quickly takes your mind off any incongruities in décor. Special lunches for $6–$8 are exceptionally ample and well prepared, while a three-course dinner (the *à la carte* menu is the same all day) will run about $17 per person. An Adriatic casserole of mussels and shrimp with potatoes and rice is a meal unto itself, as is veal with scallions, mushrooms, and peppers in a light white wine sauce. Most pastas are homemade and offered with your choice of sauces.

Le Pot Aux Roses, 185 St. Paul West. A high tin-ceilinged luncheon spot with sandwiches ($4–$5), quiches, salads and juices. Also excellent for relaxing over a cup of coffee.

Continuing the tour of the St. Paul commercial district:

Hector Lamonte, Inc., 92 St. Paul East, for saddlery and leather goods.

Les Artisans du Meuble Quebecois, 88 St. Paul East, with furniture-building kits, French lace curtains by the yard and in finished sizes, pottery, enamel, quilts, etc.

Marquis de Sade, 40 St. Paul East, a large, airy,

windowed disco and jazz restaurant bar that comes to life after 10:00 P.M. Usually no admission charge.

Chez Brandy, 407 St. Jean Baptiste (facing onto St. Paul), another late-night singles hangout with an active local bar scene and sofas for those who meet their match to chat.

Le Guilde Graphique, 9 St. Paul West, a frame shop also selling an interesting collection of modern Quebec prints and graphics.

La Boite A Cadeaux and Le Bourlinguer, 363 St. Francois-Xavier, the former with a pricey but excellent assortment of household accessories primarily for kitchen and bath, the latter a neat little café for light snacks or lunch.

Take St. Francois-Xavier down toward the waterfront, turning west again on William Street. Before you will be the Youville Stables, which, while they were never actually stables, now house offices and a steakhouse, Gibby's, with a beautiful inner courtyard that is a perfect setting for drinks in summer. The buildings date from 1825—1860, as does the red brick edifice at the center of Place d'Youville—once the Old Montreal fire station.

Gibby's 298 Place D'Youville (282-1837), is best known for its grilled meats and the size of its portions. The restaurant itself is exceptionally pleasant—fieldstone walls, beamed ceilings, and polished pine floors. Lunches from $5–$8 and *à la carte* dinners ($20 and up) share the steaks-and-chops orientation, with a few fish and seafood offerings almost a second thought. The restaurant seats up to 300, though the maze of small dining rooms keep a certain level of intimacy—and meats arrive grilled as requested.

Wind your way up St. Pierre Street, left onto St. Paul, and left again up St. Francois-Xavier, to Saint

Sulpice Seminary, the oldest building in Montreal (begun in 1685 and first used in 1712). Right onto Notre Dame Street brings you to Place d'Armes on your left and, unmistakably, Notre Dame Cathedral on your right. Place d'Armes was the site of a battle between the French and the Iroquois Indians in 1644. A monument in the plaza commemorates Sieur de Maisonneuve's slaying of the Indian chief. Looking around the square the contrasts of old and new once again scream out: The classical revival Bank of Montreal to the northwest; the International Bank—Montreal's first skyscraper; the Art-Deco Banque Royale; and Notre Dame itself.

As it stands now, last rebuilt in 1829 under architect James O'Donnell, Notre Dame is one of the first Gothic Revival churches in Canada, and one that became a model for the construction of other Catholic churches in Quebec. The twin towers, standing 227 feet high, were finished in the 1840s, the lavish interior more than thirty years later, with the current stained-glass windows added in 1929. Guided tours of the interior are available May through October (849–1070). Leaflets are available in the church for self-guided tours.

The little side street of St. Sulpice offers two small boutiques and one of two favorite Polish restaurants in Montreal (the other is on Prince Arthur).

Stash's Café Bazaar, 461 St. Sulpice (861–2915), offers inexpensive, hearty, and most appetizing blintzes, dumplings, sausages, and the like. Décor is early hand-me-down and good-humored. There's nothing above $5 at lunch, or $8 at dinner, and spending $20 for two will burst your stomach before your wallet. Closed Christmas through New Year's.

Complete your circle of the Old City by returning to Champs de Mars via Notre Dame Street. En route, note the highly modern new justice building at the corner of St. Lawrence, the construction of which prompted a tightening of rules governing the addition and/or alteration of any building in the Old City; the Cultural Affairs Ministry (between St. Gabriel and St. Vincent); and the Old Courthouse, diagonally opposite the Cultural Affairs Ministry. Just off Notre Dame at 444 St. Gabriel is Centre de ceramique Poterie Bonsecours—truly the finest crafts gallery in the city. The ceramic and glass pieces are collector's items, most of them affordable yet highly stylized and individual. The gallery also sponsors demonstrations and workshops.

Note: You may wish to follow a more circuitous route back toward the station, as the side streets are filled with fine restaurants and boutiques as well as examples of recent housing renovations. One of the more interesting of the latter is the warehouse-cum-condominium off St. Sulpice at Le Royer Street; its (hoped-for) success will no doubt have a very strong influence on to what degree further redevelopment of the neighborhood is undertaken.

St. Denis—
Prince Arthur

The St. Denis area, which for our purposes takes in Prince Arthur and Duluth Streets along with St. Lawrence (St. Laurent) Blvd., offers the greatest concentration of ethnic diversity in all of Montreal.

By day, St. Lawrence is an important shopping district, with scores of European, Oriental, Indian, and Caribbean shops selling exotic foods—packaged and freshly prepared—household goods, clothing and the like. This is a rare, largely ungentrified strip where signs are as likely to be in some Slavic language or Chinese as in French or English. Old-fashioned hardware stores stuff what must be one of everything they sell into their windows, a layer of dust attesting to the given emporium's longevity. The occasional boutique-style shop between the others stands as a harbinger of change that will no doubt come.

As bustling as St. Lawrence is by day, it is desolate at night except for a handful of restaurants spread

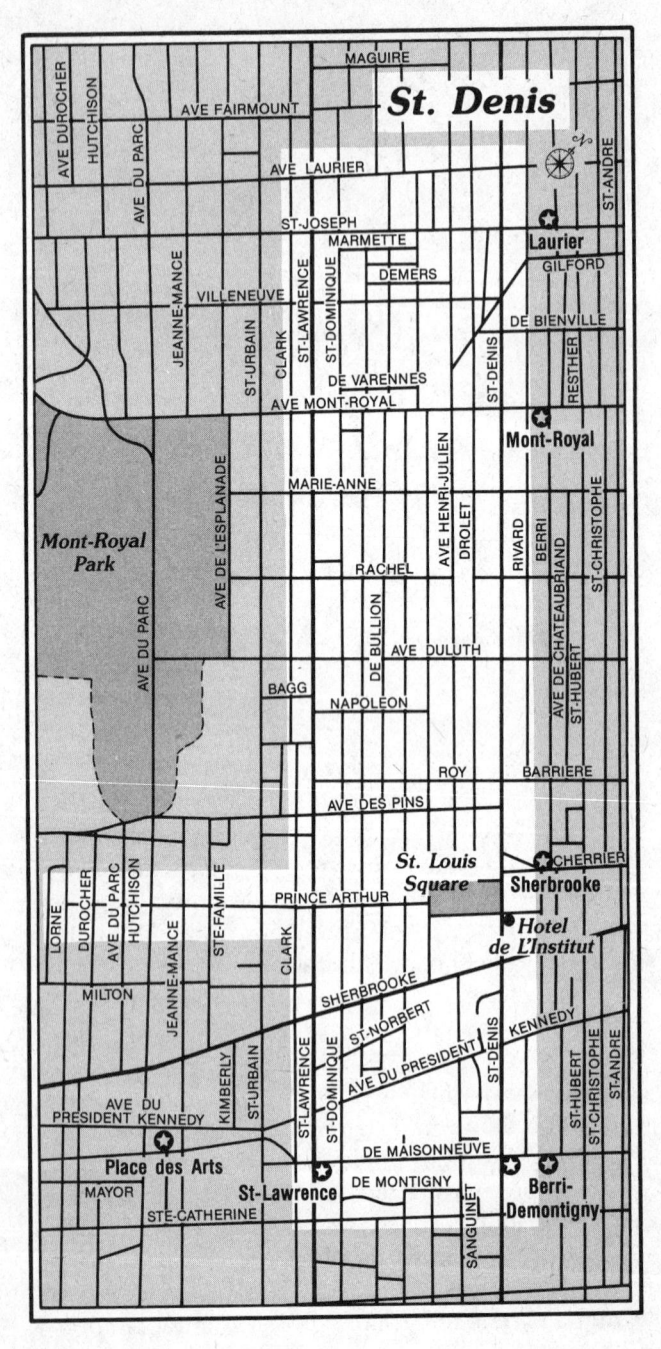

ST. DENIS—PRINCE ARTHUR 64

widely apart—while St. Denis, Prince Arthur, and Duluth Streets take on an exuberance that is exhilarating. These latter streets are calm, though somewhat populated, during the day, but by 5:00 P.M. they start to take on a life that is very specially their own. Each has its own character and appeal, though "popularly priced" is the common denominator. The "bring your own bottle" movement has really taken hold in the restaurants that line Prince Arthur and Duluth.

While we'll suggest a circular walking tour that covers at least a little of each section of the St. Denis area, you may wish to concentrate on a particular stretch at a time or link them into a day-long tour that starts with fresh-baked rolls and coffee on St. Lawrence, stops on upper St. Denis for a light lunch, and culminates with dinner on Prince Arthur. Re-energized, you can even finish the night off dancing to the wee hours back on St. Denis.

St. Lawrence, the official dividing line between east and west Montreal, is the heart of the city's old-line ethnic heritage. When such distinctions held, English-speaking Montrealers resided primarily to the west while Francophones dwelled to the east. Settled largely by Jews fleeing the Russian pogroms in the 1880s, the street retains much of the flavor of those early settlers despite a migration of the city's Jewish community northwestward.

North of Sherbrooke and as far as Duluth, there are Jewish-style bakeries, delis, and even a steakhouse; Portuguese, Czech, and Polish clothing and food stores; shops for Caribbean and Ukrainian handicrafts; bridal gowns and fine linens from western Europe; and Indian herbs and spices. Accents are thick. Well-dressed passersby mumble at you, offering watches, gold chains, and leather pocket books. A sign of the times: a revival movie house, Le Cinema Parallele (No. 3684), is tucked behind a tiny coffeehouse, Café Melies, where a bare-footed patron is likely to sit at the window reading philosophy books and sipping expresso. The films? "The Grand Illusion," "Triumph of the Will," "Burden of Dreams," while sandwiches and salads are only $2–$3. Students and artists are moving in to take advantage of a central location and low rents. The neighborhood will be a-changin'.

Montreal Hebrew Delicatessen & Steak House (No. 3895) has been known simply as Schwartz's since 1927, but the Schwartz family sold to a Greek family some years back—passing on their secret recipe for smoked-meat sandwiches. Kosher-style but non-kosher corned beef and pastrami are available as well, as are most other deli staples.

Moishe's (No. 3961; 845-1696) is where you go for steaks in this neighborhood, improbable as that may sound. The place is tacky and kitschy despite all efforts at modernity—Moishe's first opened in 1938—and every mealtime is all-hell-break-loose time. Call it "festive," if you will. The portions are hefty, the beef first-rate, the herring and salmon pickled on the premises, bread and (seemingly) lead-stuffed pastries homemade. Full lunches run to $8.50; *à la carte* main dishes to $13.50.

Early each summer there's a street festival sponsored by the Village St.-Laurent trade association, with merchants bringing their food and wares into the street for sampling. There's a swimming pool open at the old public bathhouse (No. 3950). The nearby synagogue still in use at Bagg and Coloniale dates back to the 1920s.

St. Denis south of Sherbrooke is a strange hybrid. The street scene is that of older teens and young 20s, punkish looking, slightly stoned and hanging out on stoops more than at the *terrasses*. Le Commensal (No. 2115) is a vegetarian restaurant selling salads at a penny a gram (along with soups, casseroles, and desserts) that for all its good intentions (and well-prepared food) can't quite shake its image as a holdout from the hippie era. (No credit cards.)

The bars—Picasso, Le Faubourg, and Kitsch offer a combination of drinking and disco dancing, the music loud, the patrons far neater (though still young) than on the street. The restaurants attract a slightly older crowd that's still better dressed. The most popular of the latter is Le Bistro St. Denis (No. 1738).

The pretty Victorian La Côte A Baron (No. 2070), has a long wood bar, backyard garden for more privacy, and reasonably priced bistro food.

The trendy Le Jardin St. Denis (No. 1615), which retains a first-class reputation (and prices) for its unusual souffles despite what most agree has been a decline in recent years.

The chocolate-laced desserts at the tiny café La Brioche Lyonnaise Ltee (No. 1593) are a treat anytime but the restaurant upstairs (same name) is one of Montreal's top exponents of nouvelle cuisine: Cold raspberry soup, guinea hen on figs, wild mushroom pate. No liquor license, so bring your own but be prepared for a lavish feast. $80 for two.

The glass-enclosed Grand Café (No. 1720) is probably the largest of the nightspots along this leg of St. Denis; it spotlights New Orleans jazz and drinks, though bistro food is most certainly available.

Unprepossessing in the midst of all the commotion is **Hotel Saint-Denis** (No. 1254, Montreal H2X 3G6; 514-849-0342), with 60 inexpensive (doubles $35-$45) but acceptably clean rooms. This is a noisy street at night, however, so don't be hasty signing in during the quiet mid-afternoon hours.

Crossing Sherbrooke going north, St. Denis stretches out. The restaurants and bars aren't right on top of one another, and there are galleries, boutiques, crafts shops, bookstores—much for browsing. The pedestrian traffic thins out, too, making it easy to walk as far north as Mount Royal Avenue on one side of the street and back down the other (about a mile in each direction) without getting bored. St. Denis here is a little further along in the way of gentrification than St. Lawrence Blvd., but the mix of the arts-oriented, high-tech, and young professionals is what makes the area distinctive.

Entering **Hotel de l'Institut,** 3535 Saint Denis, Montreal H2X 3P1 (514–873–4163) is reminiscent of entering a college dorm—and for good reason: this is a hotel school open to the public. Housekeeping, general services, and food are all excellent, though, and even more so when you consider that doubles go for about $68 a night. Nothing here is lavish, but everything and everybody are earnest and well-meaning. Reservations are a must well in advance (a month or more) as the price, ambience, and location make this a very popular resting place.

Heading north on St. Denis, the following are typical of the shops and restaurants lining the route. Note also the generously planted tubs of flowers in summer, and the small rings of flowers around the upper part of lampposts.

La Medina (No. 3464), with its native Moroccan décor, features a wide variety of couscous, including some without meat, for $9.50–$12.50.

Le Triskell (No. 3470) has an even wider variety of Breton crêpes served in a cheerful setting of red-and-white checkered tablecloths and curtains, wood-paneled walls, and native memorabilia. Dishes range from $2.50 to $5.25 and make for an excellent light lunch.

Tango (No. 3903) features Art-Deco furnishings and decorative pieces.

L'Express (No. 3927). Reservations are honored —and a must, though 45–60 minutes at the spectacular stainless steel bar is time well spent observing a wonderfully trendy scene that's lively, fun, friendly, with some of the best food on St. Denis. Bistro with a nouvelle twist comes in the form of noodles with three kinds of wild mushrooms and slivers of duck. That alone is worth the trip. Reasonable, too: $25 for two with drinks and tip.

Aubes (No. 3935) is a gallery specializing in contemporary expressionist Canadian artists.

Scientifique (No. 3965) appropriately enough specializes in books and toys with a scientific orientation.

Metamorphose (southwest corner of Duluth) has weavings, pottery, handmade toys, decorative tiles, and other craft work.

Bronx (No. 4077) offers clothing for the well-heeled punk set—i.e., hand-painted Keds sneakers just don't come cheap. Ditto for Gomina (No. 4228).

Franc jeu (No. 4140) is a colorful, broadly stocked toy store emphasizing the educational aspect of play but without forgetting that play is also *fun*.

Le Goût du Viet Nam (No. 4157) is one of the best representatives of Vietnamese cooking to be found in Montreal. With its French as well as Oriental influences, this is a surprisingly light cuisine marked by very subtle seasoning and seemingly greaseless frying. Vegetable or seafood rolls are a must for appetizers, and there is an excellent selection of duck, fish, meat, and vegetarian dishes. $20 for two will buy you more food than you probably ought to eat—though you're likely to finish it all.

Claire Belzil (No. 4269) doesn't offer anything cheap, but the imported clothes, mostly by French and Italian designers, are tasteful and practical.

Dixversions (No. 4361) is a high-tech furniture store with well-selected lines.

Still farther north, around the 4800 blocks, new galleries have been opening (and closing) as St. Denis continues its expansion.

Prince Arthur can be reached from St. Denis by walking through St. Louis Square (St. Louis Street is one block north of Sherbrooke). The section from Laval Avenue at the western end of the square to St. Lawrence Blvd. is closed to motorists; in summer the cobblestoned mall becomes one large outdoor *terrasse*.

This is definitely a fun area to visit—the night-life scene in summer, with street performers at every corner and local residents wending their way through the throngs with their bicycles. It's the best entertainment in town, but it is not especially noteworthy for what you'll be served in overcrowded restaurants where everyone fights for the window tables.

With a few noteworthy exceptions, the restaurants here are all Greek. Some posing as Italian, with all due respect to pasta on their menus, give themselves away with their selections of appetizers (stuffed grape leaves, cucumbers in yogurt) and desserts (baklava, of course). Décor is as undistinguishable from one place to the next as are the restaurant names and menus. You can count on La Casa Grecque, Le Gourmet Grecque, La Cabane Grecque, and La Taverne Grecque to be serving shish-kabob, moussaka, and other standard Greek fare in generous helpings that may or may not be hot and are almost never particularly interestingly executed. You can similarly count on each place being wood-paneled with scores of hanging plants, antique oak pieces in modern settings, wood tables, plastic coverings atop green linen cloths, caned chairs (some are admittedly upholstered), and glass-encloseable *terrasses.* The checks will be $10–$12 per person and in most instances you are urged to bring your own wine or beer obtainable at nearby groceries. (There is some backlash to this trend, with locals arguing that the establishments serving alcohol can afford to offer better food.)

Whatever the restaurants' individual merits, the growth of commerce on this street has served as something of a catalyst for encouraging young professionals to restore period houses throughout the neighborhood (the streets around St. Louis Square) and to help redevelop an ethnically diverse area that was bordering on the shabby. The artists and craftspeople who first opened their galleries, boutiques, and second-hand clothing stores here have been forced to move because of higher rents, but the net effect has been to create an area that most Montrealers

71   ST. DENIS—PRINCE ARTHUR

look at as an excellent place to spend an inexpensive night out. There are certainly also a few standouts among the restaurants and bars, and these are worth singling out.

Pizza Mella (No. 107) can be found by looking for the longest line on Prince Arthur. The line extends from a brass and smoked-glass-fronted two-tiered legitimately Italian restaurant. Individual size (and larger) pizzas come with any number of extra toppings, are served piping hot, and are really the only thing to order here. Most small pies are $4–$5 each. Across the street is the similarly popular Pasta Mella.

Vol de Nuit (No. 14) is unquestionably the most attractive spot on Prince Arthur. A disco-bar, its ads promise "doctors, students, poets, lovers, businessmen"—and that is in fact the clientele, who come to relax, dance, converse, or dream (to paraphrase the barowner's own words) in director's chairs set in a large oak-walled room decorated with art-deco lamps, stuffed cartoon-like busts and sculptures. Very conducive to meeting new friends or for chatting with old ones.

Vespucci (No. 124) stands out if only for all the white tables and chairs out front in summer, and for its somewhat fancier-than-average interior. The menu is also a little more serious than most in this area, and its prices reflect it: veal and fish run $11–$15, pastas $4.50–$8.50. Everything is prepared fresh, though, and Vespucci counts for dining rather than merely eating.

Le Bal St. Louis (No. 80) is a bar that serves bagels. (Need more be said?)

As you walk along Prince Arthur itself, don't forget to look up and down the side streets. The roofs and trim are a bright, bold claim to individuality, the winding wrought-iron staircases a classic device of Montreal architecture that saves room on the interior of so many homes.

Duluth Street is well on its way to becoming another Prince Arthur. It, too, will probably be closed to traffic at some point, allowing some very attractive Greek, French, and Vietnamese restaurants to expand onto the sidewalks. So far, the fact that Duluth isn't fully developed means that there are a few more galleries and boutiques still in residence, and that the restaurants have to work a little harder to attract patrons both in way of décor and menu. The only fear is that the more successful are likely to serve as role models for newcomers—and the same type of duplication that mars Prince Arthur will take hold on Duluth.

For now (and with the understanding that restaurants in up-and-coming districts come and go with sadly predictable haste), the most noteworthy are La Terasse Duluth, with etched glass outside and Victorian interior, serving a mix of Italian and Greek specialties (dinners average $12) and Les Papillions des Rhodes, a straightforward Greek restaurant with butterflies gently floating on the wallpaper. For general exploring, Duluth Street can be walked about a half mile from St. Lawrence to Lafontaine Park.

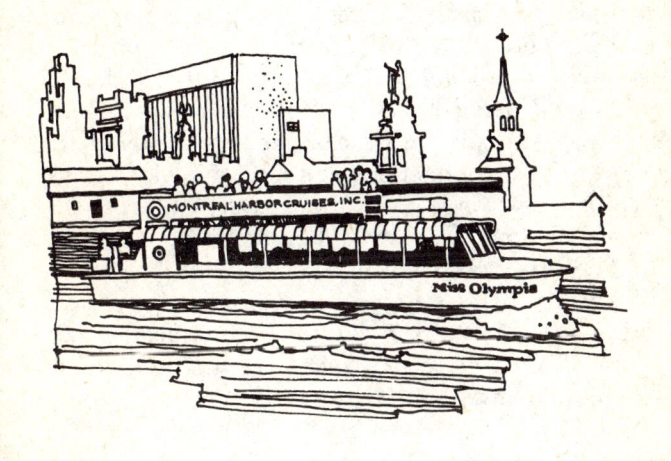

Other City Excursions

Designed by American landscape architect Frederick Law Olmstead, Mount Royal Park is a source of year-round recreation opportunities, as well as having the best natural views of Montreal. Côté des Neiges Road cuts through the park, making access simple by car or bus (No. 115 from Sherbrooke and Guy; or the No. 11 from the Mount Royal Métro station). Beaver Lake is used for ice skating in winter, and for sailing model boats in summer. Cross-country skiing and snowshoeing are popular when there's enough of the powdery white stuff, while jogging, strolling, and picnicking are popular in warmer weather.

Snacks—soft drinks and hot dogs—are available at the chalet near the peak and at Beaver Lake, but your best bet on the right day (or night—Montreal's reputation for safety includes after-dark hours in the park) is to brown bag it. The city's numerous *boulangeries* or *charcuteries* will pack meals of salads, or cheese, pâtés, and bread in a basket or bag complete with necessary utensils, drinks, and paper goods. Near the No. 115 bus stop mentioned above, one block south of Sherbrooke on Mathieu Street, is Au Bon Croissant, a combination *boulangerie* and pastry shop. The foods in the display cases are as good to eat as they are to look at. For deli-style sandwiches described in greater detail in the Downtown chapter, stop at Beauty's, 93 Mount-Royal Ave. West, which is a few blocks west of the Mount Royal Métro.

The Botanical Garden and Olympic Park are a good combination for a half-day's excursion. The Pie-IX Métro station lets you out at the main stadium, while Métro Viau is a bit closer to the Velodrome. The former is the nearest to the Garden.

The 180-acre Botanical Garden boasts more than 20,000 species, many housed in the nine interconnected greenhouses on the grounds. An hour-and-a-half guided tour is available much of the year via tram for 25 cents. No eating or drinking is allowed in the groves, the individual garden areas, or near the fountain, though wedding parties are permitted to have photo sessions on Saturdays. In June you'll see quite a few brides and grooms taking advantage of the spectacular setting. The summer-long *Les Floralies Internationales de Montreal* flower show held on Ile Notre-Dame is sponsored by the Botanical Garden. The Garden is open daily from 9:00 A.M. to 6:00 P.M. Phone 252-1171.

Olympic Park—and the 1973 Montreal Olympics generally—are the source of considerable acrimony within the city. Though Montreal's mayor has been reelected several times despite the money the city lost on the games and on subsequent maintainence of the stadiums (ditto for Expo '67), the local population has mixed feelings about the notion of completing the office tower from which a removeable roof for Olympic Stadium would be suspended. The mayor sees the tower as a potential symbol for the city; many Montrealers apparently recognize the value of such a landmark but hesitate over spending money on it when there appears to be little need for the space and little likelihood of the project ever recouping the necessary investment.

It is with that background in mind that the hour-and-a-half tour of Olympic Park is particularly interesting. Of course, no mention is made of the $5 million lost annually in keeping the 70,000-capacity Stadium (home of Montreal's Expos baseball team), the Velodrome—a natural wood roller skating and bicycling track—and the six-pool swimming complex afloat.

The facilities *are* exceptional, however, from architectural and design standpoints. There are no interior beams or blocked-view seats. All three are state-of-the-art in terms of media hook-ups (underwater windows for televising swim meets, for instance, as well as all the necessary cable for other electronic reporting) and skylights in the Velodrome permitting 70% light penetration.

While the Stadium and Velodrome are of interest from an academic standpoint even when there are no games or races on—and from the sporting enthusiasts' angle when there are—the heated 25×50-meter competition pool in the swimming complex is open for free public use during specified hours all year round. There are locker and shower facilities and a wading pool for children.

The guides at Olympic Park will dazzle you with statistics as they stroll with you through the various buildings, and you are likely to be impressed. At press time, though, it was unclear what would happen when the moratorium on construction of the Stadium tower is up. You might want to pose that issue to the guides

OTHER EXCURSIONS 76

when they ask if there are any questions. For less complicated questions call 252-4737.

The Islands of Ste.-Helene and Notre Dame were used to house the 1967 Montreal World Expo, the latter built especially for the occasion. Today, a few of the pavilions remain and are used for summer exhibits under the catch-all name "Man and His World." The Museum of Contemporary Art is here, too, which seems to have assured it a position of unrivaled obscurity. While the Man and His World exhibits are of no more than passing interest (to check on the current exhibit at the Museum call 873-2878), time on the islands can be well spent swimming in the municipal pools, strolling the gardens between the pavilions (the *Les Floralies* show mentioned above), visiting the Vieux (old) Fort, the Alcan Aquarium, and the amusement park, La Ronde. Picnic tables in beautifully shaded areas abound. And auto racing fans take note: The Canada Grand Prix is held the second week in June at a track on Notre Dame Island. Theatre de la Poudriere hosts dance companies and concerts during the summer months.

Ile Ste.-Helene is accessible via Métro to the Ste.-Helene Island stop. Once on the island, a series of *balades,* or trams, carry you between points and to and from the neighboring Notre Dame Island. Cost for the *balades* is 50 cents per ride. The islands can also be reached by auto or bicycle via the Jacques Cartier Bridge.

In summer, you may want to carry swimsuits and towels to the island, for there are three large public swimming pools just to the left of the Métro station. Open 11:00 A.M. to 8:00 P.M.; admission has in the past been free until 4:00 P.M. weekdays, and never more than $1.25, including locker fee.

Clearly marked signs will lead you from the Métro or the pools to the Old Fort, which is literally that: a protected area that was intended as an arsenal when built in 1822. An indoor museum tells of life in Canada during the seventeenth and eighteenth centuries through displays of artifacts, models, furnishings, and other items. In addition, there are "military" parades in full costume that recreate the *Compagnie Franche de la Marine,* a French batallion that was stationed in North America from the 1680s to 1760. Similarly, there is a re-enactment of Fraser Highlander marching, complete with bagpipes and drums. The museum is open all year round, though the parades, which are a colorful and entertaining spectacle for children, are staged in summer only from 11:00 A.M. to 4:30 P.M. Admission fees are nominal (about $1.50 for adults, $1 for children). The restaurant Le Festin du Gouverneur (879–1141) serves a set menu that's quite secondary to the costumed Samuel de Champlain and his singing brethren who help make a party of every utensil-less meal. (About $20 per adult, $12 per child.) Call to check the sittings.

On Ile Ste.-Helene between the Métro stop and La Ronde is Helene de Champlain Restaurant, named, as is the island, for Samuel Champlain's wife, serving not inexpensive lunch from 11:30 A.M. to 2:30 P.M. and dinner from 5:30 to 11:00 P.M. You enter a large lounge and bar area with small tables for cocktails; the atmosphere is clubby, as though you should be arriving to watch the (nonexistent) yacht races on the St. Lawrence out back. The downstairs dining room overlooks a beautiful rose garden, while the upstairs hall has an unobstructed view of the water. The setting is definitely what sets the restaurant apart. The menu emphasizes seafood, but has something for everyone, even if the cooking is nothing out of the ordinary. The clientele is on the older side. For reservations: 395-2424.

From here it's a pleasant wooded walk to both the aquarium and La Ronde. Though the aquarium has been undergoing renovations in recent years the Alcan is still very much worth a visit. The friendliest of penguins greet all visitors as soon as they've paid their $2 admission; from there it's a series of tanks and display cases nicely laid out and with just enough information to satisfy normal curiosity. The aquarium is open from May through Labor Day, paralleling La Ronde. For hours, call 872-4656.

La Ronde is an amusement park complete with colorful rides, cotton candy, staged shoot-outs, haunted houses, wild west shows, banjo music, and plenty of food stalls and restaurants. Both the monorail and a cablecar give great overhead views of the park itself as well as of the Montreal skyline (the cablecar, however, lets you off at the other end of the park and you must wait in line again if you want a round trip).

Obviously this is a family attraction, and the kids in tow are young—until the later weeknight hours, when teens and young adults tend to dominate. There are various tickets that offer admission and rides, the most popular being $10 per adult, $7 per child, or a $25 family ticket good for two adults and two children, with additional kids $5 apiece. These tickets offer unlimited rides, mini-golf, and entry to other attractions.

The city has yet to figure out just what to do with the remnants of Expo '67—and it's obvious. The exhibits at Man and His World, which are housed in the Quebec Pavillion, change each year. The 1983 theme, for example, was "Communication Is Life," with displays by various governmental agencies and private corporations built largely around the role of computers in communications, farming, entertainment, and politics. "Handicraft activities" consisted primarily of a few artists selling their not terribly original or interesting work. Free entertainment was varied. Execution of the entire concept, however, was uninspired, to put it gently.

So long as weather permits, it would be a pity to be in Montreal without getting out on the water. Harbor cruises run daily from mid-May through the end of September. Lasting between one and three hours, and costing $5–$10 per adult ($3 per child), there are sunset cruises, trips with dance band and bar, and even a Sunday brunch cruise. Most feature recorded narration that lasts about half an hour and which provides a little bit of Montreal's maritime history. You board the cruise ships from a gangplank extended from the *Ville Marie II*—a large ship docked at Victoria Pier at the foot of Berri Street in Old Montreal. *That* ship has a nightly buffet from 6:30 to 8:00 P.M. with live bands and dancing until the late hours. For tickets: Montreal Harbor Cruises Inc., P.O. Box 1085, Place d'Armes, Montreal H2Y 3J6 (514-842-3871).

For those with something more rugged in mind, trips through the Lachine Rapids are also available. (The rapids got their name when early explorers believed they'd come upon China.) One excursion, which is relatively tame but conveniently located, departs from the same Victoria Pier as the cruises every two hours throughout the day beginning at 9:00 A.M. The rides, in motorized jet-boats rather than the usual rafts, last about an hour and a half. The $25 price ($20 for children) includes rain gear. Advance reservations are accepted, and necessary after Labor Day.

Raft trips through rougher portions of the rapids are offered by Voyageur Lachine (514-637-3566) from mid-June to mid-September at $10-$15 per person depending on time and day of departure (weekday mornings are cheapest). Minimum age requirement is 14, and some experience in water sports is suggested —which is some indication that this is a serious rapids ride. The company provides life vest, guides, paddles, and shuttle service back from the finishing point; you should bring towel, swimsuit, sneakers and (when appropriate) windbreaker. To get to the pier, take bus No. 191 from the Lionel Groulex Métro station to the foot of 32nd Ave.

Shopping

Given the favorable exchange rate Americans enjoy in Canada—about 30 percent at the time of this writing—and Montreal's bi-cultural cosmopolitanism, shopping is a delight here no matter what you may be seeking. As a member of the British Commonwealth, the array of goods from other Commonwealth countries is substantial; as a largely Francophile culture, there is an equally strong favoring of French designs. Don't leave your shopping until Sunday, however, as almost everything is closed (a few exceptions will be cited below).

Ste. Catherine Street is the center for department store shopping, with Ogilvy's, Simpsons, Eaton's, and La Baie within a few blocks of each other in the heart of downtown, and with Holt Renfrew on Sherbrooke near the Ritz-Carlton Hotel. The other shops on Ste. Catherine are of the boutique variety and vary widely in the quality of goods; on Sherbrooke between the Ritz-Carlton and Guy Street to the west, and along the sidestreets in the Crescent Street area (Montagne,

La Baie, Ste. Catherine St. West and Phillips Square, is the flagship outlet of a chain that emphasizes the French side of Quebec tastes. It is the most stylish and trendy of the Ste. Catherine stores and appeals to a young clientele.

Simpson's, 977 Ste. Catherine Street West, and **Ogilvy's,** 1307 Ste. Catherine Street West, are at the opposite end of the spectrum, in terms of merchandise and customers. The specialty at Simpson's is imported British Commonwealth goods. Extensive selections of Liberty silk and cotton, Irish Moygashel linen, Royal Doulton and Wedgewood China, and Waterford crystal are available. At Ogilvy's, it's the Scottish influence that is most apparent, what with a bagpiper marching through the store between noon and 12:15 P.M. daily, the kilted elevator men and the tartan design that is the store's insignia. Having begun as a linen shop in 1866, Ogilvy's continues to offer much in the way of white goods, though fashion and antiques are also featured.

Eaton's, 677 Ste. Catherine Street West, also part of a 65-store national chain, falls somewhere between the two extremes. This is a full-line department store that's trying to build a more contemporary image by introducing a boutique-like set-up in its fashion departments. Most labels here bear the names of Canadian designers largely unfamiliar in the U.S.

Holt Renfrew, 1300 Sherbrooke Street West, is best-known for its furs—furs having been central to Montreal's development since the times of its earliest "discoverers," and with 80% of the nation's fur industry located in the city. The third floor is devoted entirely to furs, while the rest of the store is given over to other fashion items.

SHOPPING

The first thing most Montrealers tell you about their famed Underground City is that the concept is not original to them, but dates back to Leonardo da Vinci. Da Vinci would no doubt have marvelled over I.M. Pei's design for the first segment of the contemporary interpretation of his dream: Place Ville Marie. The cruciform building that towers above the underground shopping arcade is possibly the most striking in all of Montreal, and the arcade itself offers congestion-free access to stores of every type—and more.

In all, there are eight miles of Underground City divided essentially into six clusters of stores, boutiques, restaurants, and cafés. The most important is the series connecting **Place Ville Marie, Place Bonaventure,** and **Place du Canada.** Almost 300 shops and 20 restaurants are located along these climate-controlled "streets," and there is access to the Queen Elizabeth, Bonaventure, and Château Champlain hotels. The Montreal Tourist Bureau points out that the only thing missing is a hardware store, but many hardware items can even be found in the kitchen and bath boutiques, of which there are many.

The six distinct areas are linked by Métro stops, meaning that Montrealers (or tourists) can pretty much avoid the blizzarding snows or blistering heat whether they wish to shop, attend the theater or opera at Place des Arts, go to the movies, dine or—relief at last—collapse back at the hotel.

About half the 150 stores at Place Bonaventure are fashion boutiques featuring all the latest in designer clothes. The latest addition to this particular arcade, Le Viaduc, is brimming with international goods in a bazaar-like atmosphere.

The most exclusive of the Underground City haunts for such apparel is the **Westmount Square Shopping Center,** near Alexis Nihon Plaza (Métro line 1 to the Atwater terminal in Westmount). Here the labels will read Cardin, Larouche, Hermes, and

Courreges, the store personnel will be most helpful, and the crowds even at peak shopping periods will be less overbearing than downtown.

Place Desjardins, the multi-leveled shopping center across from Place des Arts and below the Meridien Hotel, is worth a visit if only from the architectural standpoint. It is spacious, airy, and appears at first to house only a few stores on each tier. The corridors extend out from the central core, however, and all told there are some hundred shops and another twenty restaurants in the complex. A hanging wood sculpture adds drama to the atrium effect, while TV shows are broadcast live from a small stage on the main concourse that is also given over to non-televised live entertainment.

For designer fashions not part of the Underground City, **Claire Belzil,** 4269 St. Denis St., is eminently worth checking out, as are the boutiques on Laurier St. in the Outremont district.

As a city very proud of both its heritage and its ability to keep up with the times, Montreal is excellent hunting ground for antique collectors as well as those seeking out the latest in high-tech. Especially appealing to those whose taste runs to North American oak and pine furniture and the Victorian accents provided by lamps, mirrors, and decorative pieces, is the area affectionately known as **Attic Row.** Following Notre Dame Street west of Peel, through a low-rent but unthreatening stretch of town, you'll find store after store of "collectibles," ranging from junkyard rejects to very fine refinished tables, chests, and armoires. This is where young Montreal couples, looking to furnish on a budget, head; as with antiques purchased anywhere, items certified by the dealer to be more than 100 years old can be brought back to the U.S. duty free.

Also on the funkier side of antique hunting—and,

ironically, *the* area for high-priced high-tech, but more on that shortly—is the St. Denis area north of Sherbrooke. **Tango** (No. 3903) is a fine little hole-in-the-wall of a shop with Art-Deco pieces. **La Remise** (No. 3844) specializes in restored pine. And **Kaleidoscope,** (No. 3842) features jewelry, lamps, and Oriental collectibles. In summer, the Sunday flea market on the pier at the foot of Place Jacques Cartier in the Old City is a good place for rummaging.

More "serious" antiquing—English and French furniture of the eighteenth and nineteenth centuries, and Oriental *objets d'art* of even earlier times—is to be found concentrated along Sherbrooke west of the Ritz-Carlton Hotel and on the sidestreets between Sherbrooke and Ste. Catherine. **Antiquités Crescent,** 2137 Crescent, specializes in pre-1850s Empire, Charles X, and Louis Philippe-period furniture. English China and French and Chinese porcelain are the specialties at **China Shop Antiques,** 2148 Mackay. Eighteenth-century Quebec furniture is to be found in the Old City at **Bonsecours Antiques,** 441 St. Claude Street. **MQ Antiques,** 180 St. Paul St. West, also in the Old City, offers reproductions of nineteenth-century designs.

Handcrafted goods are available throughout the city, though if it's more than a souvenir you're after, we urge you not to get caught up in the tourist shops offering hundreds of "handmade" wood dolls or soapstone carvings. More interesting items, and better examples of these, can be purchased from legitimate crafts co-ops and shops. Among the best:

Centre de ceramique Poterie Bonsecours, 444 St. Gabriel St., in the Old City, has an outstanding collection of mostly ultra-modern pottery, glass, and ceramic sculpture, some of which are strictly decorative while others—interesting black-and-white tea sets, round-bottomed soup terrines on one visit—are for use. Some jewelry is also displayed, and there are classes and public craftmaking demonstrations available. Most of the items are also surprisingly affordable, with many in the $40–$60 range.

L'Empreinte, 272 St. Paul East, also in the Old City, is an artists' cooperative showcasing a wide variety of handicrafts—with the work of only one or two artists in a given medium represented at a time. Clothing, weaving, batik, and leather goods are available as well as pottery, jewelry, decorative tiles, and some prints and photographs.

Canada Guild of Crafts, 2025 Peel St., is a beautiful downtown shop filled with quilts, prints, masonry, silver, and blown glass, with an adjoining store devoted to Eskimo soapstone sculpture and art. Given its location, you can expect prices here to be higher than in the Old City, with most of the work more in the way of collector's pieces than for daily use.

Metamorphose, southwest corner of Duluth on St. Denis, is more of a boutique than the others mentioned, but the selection reflects taste in everything from handmade children's pull toys to weavings, wall hangings, pottery, scarves, notecards, and the like.

Centrale d'Artisant de Quebec, 1450 St. Denis, specializes in Eskimo and Quebec arts and crafts.

Bargain hunters looking for good buys on imported China and glass, including such names as Fitz & Lloyd and Boda, should head way up St. Denis St. to **Le Cache Pot** (No. 5047). Discounts are typically 25% off list—which is especially impressive when the additional 30% is knocked off for U.S. dollars.

Those seeking designer clothes at less than designer prices can go to Notre Dame St. east of McGill, one of the few areas with stores open on Sundays. You'll pick through cartons of sweaters, shirts, and pants to find your size at **Fairmart** (No. 409), where they carry Bloomingdale's seconds for women on the main floor and for men upstairs. **Tripp Distributeurs** (No. 397) has last year's Lauren, Klein and Yves St. Laurent styles. And **Faubourg Notre Dame** (No. 239) essays a hipper boutique-like image (complete with sales help), though less-familiar names.

Miscellaneous: St. Denis is the place for high-tech fashion and furnishings: **Bronx** and **Gomina,** at 4077 and 4228 St. Denis St., respectively, will appeal to punk instincts with their combination of '50s funk and '80s glitter. Stylish (in an extreme way) these clothes are; cheap they are not. Similarly, **Dixversions,** 4361 St. Denis St., is the place for hi-gloss plastic tables, operating room-like lamps, and absurd little decorative pieces.

As described in previous chapters, most of the city's art galleries are located along Sherbrooke, west of the Museum of Fine Arts, and on upper St. Denis. While a number of galleries have become established on St. Denis up around Duluth St., the newest are popping up still farther north, near the Laurier Métro station.

Two unusual toy shops are also located on St. Denis: **Franc jeu** (No. 4140), has an interesting assortment of mostly educational toys—building sets, arts and crafts supplies and traditional "learning" games. **Scientifique** (No. 3935) emphasizes, as its name suggests, scientific books and toys.

Restaurants

Montreal lays rightful claim to second place among culinary capitals in North America. It is second only to New York in general level of quality, in ethnic diversity, and in willingness to experiment. Even more so than in New York, however, you *dine* in Montreal; you don't simply "eat out." The local *croissanterie* may not offer haute cuisine, but those with a few tables in the back are likely to prepare a fresh salad to order with whatever makings are seasonally available, that reflects the enthusiasm Montrealers bring to food, even for a $3 meal.

Ironically, the best classical French restaurants in the city are regularly chided for continuing to serve canned or frozen vegetables—often when fresh ones are in season. When in doubt, ask; as the waiter begins to avert his eyes, you can expect the volume of his voice to drop as he murmurs "No," in answer to whether the asparagus offered as an appetizer is fresh. The same holds for fish, despite Montreal's being a port city. In other ways the local bounty is offered freely. When raspberries are in season late in the summer your plate will overflow with them. Indeed, generally speaking, portions are generous even in multi-course *table d'hôte* meals.

Certainly Montreal has its share of undistinguished coffeeshops and fast-food restaurants, but even when it's something quick you're after, there are alternatives—the aforementioned *croissanteries*, local *charcuteries*, and souvlaki stands. When watching the budget there are two other alternatives: make your main meal lunch, and partake of the weekday "businessmen's" specials that are offered almost everywhere for $6–$10 including appetizer, main course, dessert and coffee; then dine lightly for dinner. Or go ethnic. As in almost every city, you can dine inexpensively but heartily and well on Chinese, Greek, Polish, Indian or Vietnamese food, to name but a few. Bistros and bars also offer good dining at moderate prices, and these tend to retain a little more of the Montreal French flavor while still keeping the bill down.

Service is a part of any serious meal in Montreal. Waiters here have an excellent sense of what it means to be available to patrons, and to keep an eye on their progress through a meal without hovering over them. With a few exceptions for those restaurants demanding coat and tie for men (duly noted below), anyone neatly dressed will be served as graciously in Montreal's finest establishments as those decked out for a glamorous night on the town.

As many restaurants have been mentioned in the preceding chapters in the context of their location, the following listing is by cuisine, with some of the best places discussed anew. We begin with French—when in Rome, so to speak—and then continue alphabetically by nationality or ethnic slant.

We have tried to provide an indication of prices, but do keep several things in mind: All prices, as throughout this book, are quoted in Canadian dollars, giving U.S. citizens about a 30% edge; the businessmen's lunches are an outstanding way to sample the best restaurants in the city at better-than-reasonable prices; many restaurants offer *table d'hôte* dinners as well, which will also come out far less expensive than ordering *à la carte;* increasingly, ethnic restaurants in particular are encouraging patrons to bring their own bottle of wine or beer. Since taxes on alcohol sold to restaurants are extremely high, this can represent a considerable saving.

The *menu degustation* is another popular trend taking hold. Inaugurated by Le Fadeau's owner/chef Henri Wojcik, and now found at a number of fashionable restaurants, this is a complete dinner that is designed to provide a taste of many specially prepared dishes. It is not for those averse to trying new things; nor is it for those watching their budgets. Unlike the *table d'hôte* dinner, the *menu degustation* tends to be rather expensive (not unreasonable, given the ingredients and the special preparation involved), chosen exclusively by the chef, and must usually be ordered for everyone at the table—sometimes a day in advance.

Whether or not budgetary considerations enter into your decision-making for dining in Montreal, the real key to appreciating the experience lies in value for the money. Taking into account food, service and ambience, you will be hard pressed to find another city where you can do as well with such regularity.

Restaurants are open seven days a week, serving lunch and dinner, and accept major credit cards, unless otherwise indicated. Many, however, close for a month during the summer. Always best to call first.

French

Altitude 737, Place Ville Marie (861–3511). The view is more interesting than the food, even with a $16.50 luncheon buffet. Dinner only, Saturday.

Beaver Club, Queen Elizabeth Hotel, 900 Dorchester West (861-3511). It's difficult to classify the Beaver Club, which is one of the most formal hotel dining rooms (jacket and tie *de rigeur*) and an excellent one if somewhat schizophrenic: one part nouvelle cuisine outpost, another part traditional club-like restaurant specializing in heavy meats. Very expensive.

Café de Paris, Ritz-Carlton Hotel, 1228 Sherbrooke St. West (842-4212). Formal is an understatement here, with jackets and ties a must and a staff that goes strictly by the book. The six-course *menu degustation* was running about $40 per person at time of writing, with steep additional charges for a third of the items listed ($19.75 for pheasant; $9 for an appetizer of scallops with caviar and salmon). *A la carte* is available, too. The setting is spectacularly Parisian, but the food, while well prepared, is not up to the atmosphere or the prices. Piano music at night.

Chez La Mère Michel, 1209 Guy St. (934-0473). Classic French country style in décor and haute cuisine, Chez La Mère Michel is readily among Montreal's most consistently outstanding restaurants. The lobster soufflé Nantua is legendary, the care taken with home-grown herbs and imported fish beyond reproach. Ambience: formal and dignified; clientele: the elder aristocracy. $65 for two for dinner. Closed Sundays; dinner only Saturdays.

La Marée, 404 Place Jacques Cartier (861-9794). Described in great detail as one of the major "sights" of Old Montreal, La Marée expends as much energy in display at your table as it must behind the kitchen doors. The results are inevitably marvelous, but the atmosphere is a mite on the stuffy side. Consider that part of the "show," though, and the $90-$100 you'll spend for two won't seem quite as outrageous. Dinner only, Saturdays and Sundays.

La Petite Halle, 1425 Bishop (849-1294). The smaller, more informal version of the city's mainstay Les Halles (see below), La Petite Halle is a few steps above bistro—though cassoulet, omelets, crêpes, and sliced steak are available—and not quite a full "restaurant." In practical terms, though, you can do wonderfully well here getting first-class cuisine at very reasonable prices. Brunch on Sunday is a perfect start to the day, but the one-menu lunch or dinner carte is perfect any time. Spend from $6 to $25 per person.

Le Caveau, 2063 Victoria St. (844-1624). Whatever your budget, and no matter how heavy or light a meal you desire, Le Caveau is probably the answer. Want an intimate romantic spot? Someplace to go with the kids? A restaurant for a business meeting? Le Caveau miraculously covers all bases. The food is very, very good, if not "special." The service is friendly and the atmosphere relaxed and informal. Inexpensive dinners including salad, main course, coffee, and dessert and featuring frogs legs, lamb with endive, or salmon with leak sauce run an amazing $8-$15 and attract many students and professors from the nearby McGill University campus. An extensive *à la carte* menu is also available. Spread over three floors of a stone house one block south of Sherbrooke; the décor is French country style with brick walls, wood mantles, copper utensils, and nineteenth-century-style watercolors. Dinner only, Sundays.

Les Chenets, 2075 Bishop (844-1842). The main attraction is a $125 *menu degustation* for two, including wine and a fanciful menu previously described in some detail. Convenient and luxurious among the Crescent Street fieldstone houses.

Le Fadeau, 423 St. Claude St. (878-3959). The adventurous should definitely ask for the *menu degustation,* which is a decision that can be made without advance notice up until an hour or so before closing. The $40-per-person meal will be filled with little delights. Otherwise, the *à la carte* menu will do just fine. Comfortable and quiet, with meticulous attention to service. Dinner only, Saturdays and Sundays.

Le St. Amable, 188 St. Amable St., right off Place Jacques Cartier (866-3471). Classic French cuisine from a menu that has held to its principles and its recipes. Dinner here is an event—and count on spending as though you were paying for the theatrical flair that accompanies the meal's presentation as well as for the food itself. Dinner only, Saturdays and Sundays.

Les Halles, 1450 Crescent (844-2328), is reputed to be the finest restaurant in all of Montreal. There are problems in the timing of the meal (the kitchen moves very slowly), but none with what is eventually served. Gay market-like murals adorn the walls, the staff is friendly (if unfortunately appropriately apologetic) and the plates marvels of the chef's decorative talents. The offerings have been described previously; suffice it to say it is worth the wait . . . and the $100 a dinner for two is likely to cost. Closed Sundays; dinner only Saturdays.

Pierre de Coubertin, Four Seasons Hotel, 1050 Sherbrooke St. West (248-1110). The first thing to strike you about this quietly spectacular dining room is the space between tables, and how quiet it is. For an intimate meeting—business or romantic—you won't find better. The prices are as high as the ceiling, but they bring a fine combination of nouvelle and classical delights. There's a trio for dancing at night as well.

Rene Varaud, 705 Ste. Catherine West (843-8592). Haute cuisine in possibly the most impossible setting imagineable: a shopping mall. Situated so as to overlook the ever-busy Les Terrasses complex, Rene Varaud boasts no freezer, and ingredients flown in from all over the globe. Once in the kitchen, those ingredients are duly pampered. A mere fifty seats allows the chef to prepare most everything to order— though as you *can* imagine, you pay for the privilege. Closed Sundays; dinner only Saturdays.

Chinese

Abacus, 2144 Mackay (933-8444). This is not at all your Chinatown-type restaurant; trendy and expensive (special Imperial and Royal menus must be ordered ahead for a minimum of four people at $25 and

$30 a head), this is one of the Crescent area's jet-setty hangouts. The usually spicy Szechuan and Hunan cuisines are the order. Dinner only Saturdays and Sundays.

Elysée Mandarin, 1221 Mackay (866-5975). Mandarin dishes are not part of the menu, which spotlights Peking and Szechuan styles. Still, this worldly restaurant (come to Montreal via Paris) handles its double-spiced King crabs, veal kidneys with hot garlic sauce, and quail with herb sauce impeccably. (More standard offerings are available, too.) Individual dishes run $10-$25, but sharing is the way to order anyway. Dinner only Sundays.

Ruby Foo's, 7815 Decarie Blvd. (731-7701). A spectacle more than a restaurant. Ruby Foo's feeds 700 at a clip out of one French and one Chinese kitchen, though the fare itself is faithful to neither culture. Portions are as generous as the prices are high, the food is much better than average, and *table d'hôte* lunches and dinners keep the cost out of the stratosphere. Worth *seeing*, for sure.

For inexpensive Chinese food with more of an ethnic bent, stalk the streets of Chinatown east and west of deBleury or on St. Lawrence south of Dorchester and pick a menu that sounds interesting.

Greek

Prince Arthur St. is lined with Greek restaurants that at least appear to be owned by one person. As described in the chapter on the St. Denis district, they are uniform in menu, appearance, and mediocrity. They are fine for when you want to check out (and be a part of) the Prince Arthur scene, and you certainly won't leave any of them hungry. Go, then, with the understanding that the food isn't the main attraction.

If good Greek *food* is what you want, then head to upper Parc Avenue, north of Laurier Street. Here you'll find the local favorites in slightly disheveled surroundings but where care is taken with preparation. Easily the single most outstanding of the restaurants here is **Symposium,** 5334 Parc Ave. (274–9547), a two-leveled, slightly schizophrenic place in the heart of Greektown. Upstairs is the more mainstream half— a full menu of standard Greek fare with perfectly cooked appetizers and a broad cross-section of fresh fish and meats. There's live bouzouki music, what passes for ethnic-style décor, and a general party-like atmosphere.

To Montrealers, however, the downstairs is the *pièce de resistance.* Once you are seated, the waiter brings over a tray of the day's catch—and that's the menu. The price of your main dish is determined by the weight of your choice, measured at the fish counter which constitutes the central decorative motif, if you will. A plate of pre-selected hors d'oeuvres is brought while the fish is prepared to your specifications, and you automatically get a Greek salad, baklava, and coffee. There's a very inexpensive daily special—usually under $10 for the meal—though the other prices are always very reasonable. Reservations are a must on weekends. Dinner only Sundays.

Le Sabayon, 666 Sherbrooke West (288–0373). Full Greek dinners from $9.50 to $26.75 and a floor show complete with bellydancers, magicians, and singers lure mostly business types on expense accounts.

Indian

Le Paon, 6107 Parc Ave. (274–3317). A hole-in-the-wall storefront with genuine tandoori oven and classically prepared dishes spiced precisely as requested. Spending $10 a person here will be difficult, which offsets the trek involved in getting there. No credit cards.

Pique-Asiette, 2051 Ste. Catherine St. West (932-7141). Affiliated with the Bombay Palace chain of London, New York, and et cetera, this is a modestly priced pleasant tavern-like place with a good if not great Indian kitchen. The vegetarian Thali, built around two very different curries, is a better bet than the various tandoori offerings; and the pickled turnip appetizer is a delightful surprise.

Italian

Chez Magnani, 9245 Lajeunesse St. (387-6438). Discounting the waiters, who seem to have affected an attitude about the fact that they've been here for eons, the food at Chez Magnani is unflinchingly fresh and classically prepared. Dinners will be very reasonable at about $15 per person. Jackets are suggested. Closed Sundays; dinner only Saturdays.

La Sila, 2040 St. Denis (844-5083). Fine homemade pastas made to order and covered with light tomato or cream-based sauces are the specialty. *Table d'hôte* dinners to about $16. Closed Sundays.

Le Muscadin, 100 St. Paul West (842-0588). The luncheon specials, as discussed in the Old Montreal chapter, are an outstanding value, the veal at all times impeccable and the pastas properly *al dente,* with a choice of sauces. *A la carte* main courses about $7.50-$11. Closed Sundays.

Pizza Mella, 107 Prince Arthur (849-4680). Long lines of patrons await the individually sized pies that cost about $4-$5 depending on which of the myriad toppings you add to the basic formula. All are prepared fresh. Great for group dining.

Vespucci, 124 Prince Arthur (843-4784), is attractive and not inexpensive. The menu is heavily weighted toward veal and fish, with great pride taken in the fact that everything—including the pasta—is made to order.

Japanese

Sushi bars are popping up in the Crescent and St. Denis areas, though Japanese food is less common here than in New York or Los Angeles. Among the older Japanese establishments, **Katsura,** 2170 Montagne St. (849-1172). Granted that the food here is outstanding, but the prices are absolutely outrageous, with dinners in the $25 range (and up), and without the kind of service that such charges call for. Still, shabu shabu is a treat rarely made available—a simmering broth into which a seemingly unending flow of vegetables and meat are dipped, with a last course of noodles thrown in for the soup finale. Tempura, sushi, and sashimi are also expertly prepared. Dinner only, Saturdays and Sundays.

Jewish

. . . but not necessarily Kosher: **Beauty's,** 93 Mont Royal Ave. West (849-8883). This is a bit of New York's Lower East Side transplanted northward. Towering concoctions of salmon (lox to New Yorkers), cream cheese, onions, and tomato on sesame bagel; omelets with everything but the kitchen sink. And the best fresh orange juice in large and larger glasses. The Art-Deco and high-tech flourishes are a little trendy, perhaps, but this Beauty's offers Montreal's perfect breakfast or brunch. Watch out for lines on weekends (closed Sundays in summer). No credit cards. Those seeking kosher food should consult **Vaad Hair,** 5491 Victoria Avenue, for current listings of restaurants and grocery stores offering kosher products.

Ben's, 990 Maisonneuve Blvd. West (844-1001). Mentioned because it's something of an institution—since the early 1900s—and not for its food. Deli sandwiches and self-made fruit-flavored soda are the way to go while checking out the autographed photos of '50s and '60s stars on the walls. No credit cards.

Moishe's, 3961 St. Lawrence Blvd. (845-1696). A little confusing, as the name clearly denotes the ethnic heritage, though Moishe's is a steak house. There's nothing delicate served here, either, but if a big meal and a lot of noise are what you want, with a side order of pickled herring, that's exactly what you'll get. Dinner will run about $20 per person.

Schwartz's Montreal Hebrew Delicatessen and Steak House, 3895 St. Lawrence Blvd. (842-4813). Leave off the steak house part and this is the real thing, even if Schwartz's is now owned by Greeks. Kosher-style smoked-meat sandwiches are the specialty. Note, too, that Schwartz's is open until after midnight daily. No credit cards.

Moroccan

La Medina, 3464 St. Denis (282-0359). Pleasantly decorated with authentic Moroccan rugs and antiques, and with a separate dessert room. The menu includes a wide variety of couscous dishes, brochettes, and casseroles all very reasonably priced (most *à la carte* main courses cost under $8). Dinner only.

Menara, 256 St. Paul (861-1989). Lamb with prunes and almonds, couscous, baked fish, and the like are very reasonably priced for a center Old City location right off Place Jacques Cartier—and for a restaurant with a floor show ($3 cover charge once the bellydancing commences). Earlier in the evening Menara is a fine place for families

Polish

Stash's Cafe Bazaar, 461 St. Sulpice (861-2915). Around the corner from the Old City's Notre Dame, they serve the classic East-European crêpes stuffed with a variety of fillings, along with dumplings, sausages, cabbage rolls, and so forth.

Quebecois

Les Filles du Roy, 415 Bonsecours St. (849-3535). Waitresses in Quebec costumes and an old fieldstone house with dark, slightly dungeon-like dining rooms set the tone. Fun with children, with fare appropriate for unadventurous appetites; the food is good enough. *A la carte* main dishes at dinner average about $9-$11.

Two places where you might consider "partying" with a group of friends or perfect for a family with children are **Le Festin du Gouverneur,** Old Fort, Ste. Helene Island (879-1141) and **Le Fou Du Roi,** 2102 Montagne St. (843-7144). Both present price-fixed medieval feasts banquet style, accompanied by group singing. No eating utensils are supplied, which supposedly adds to the fun. The food is about equally uninteresting at both, the setting more "realistic," as it were, on Ste. Helene Island. The whole event is a great deal of fun if the crowd is right.

Seafood

In choosing a restaurant for seafood, keep in mind that this is the mainstay of menus in most classical and nouvelle French establishments. Among those mentioned in the listings for French restaurants above, you should definitely consider La Marée, Le St. Amable, and Les Halles. Also:

Chez Pauze, 1657 Ste. Catherine St. West (932-6118). A big, noisy place that's right out of the late '50s; good for families even if the kitchen relies too much on frozen foods and institutional sauces and dressings.

Desjardins Sea Food, 1175 Mackay St. (866-9741). A pretty setting—modern in the new wing, French country in the old—and nicely appointed tables make up for the lackluster dishes that emerge from the kitchen. Not bad, mind you, but not special, either. Dinner only, Saturdays and Sundays. Dinners $17–$20.

Le Pavillon d'Atlantique, Alcan Building on Sherbrooke at Stanley Street. Newly transplanted to these ultra modern surroundings, this long-time favorite still offers an oyster bar and some very high prices. The expense account crowd supports Le Pavillon, and while the food is good and the setting striking, the bill will be unconscionably high. Dinner only, Sundays.

Maritime Bar, Ritz Carlton Hotel, 1228 Sherbrooke St. West (842-4212). If you can hack the prices—*à la carte* main courses up to around $20—this is a beautiful restaurant eager to establish a clientele that's not as stuffy as that attending the Ritz's other dining emporiums. Though jackets and ties are required, you get a choice of thirteen Dover sole creations, among many others. Service is outstanding, as befits the environment and the cost. Dinner only, Sundays.

Steaks

Gibby's, 298 Place Youville (282–1837). Part of the Youville Stables restoration, with wood-beamed ceilings, fieldstone walls, and Old-World ambience. It would be hard not to enjoy anything ordered here—especially if you've managed a table looking out on the small green square toward the rear. Rib and sirloin steaks are the highlights (about $16–$18), though some chicken, fish, and seafood are also available.

Also, Moishe's, listed above under "Jewish."

Swiss

Alpenhaus, 1279 St. Marc (935–2285). Better on looks than food, but fun for a fondue or raclette, which are filling and inexpensive. Piano music in the, yes, Heidi Room. Dinner only, Saturdays and Sundays.

William Tell, 2055 Stanley St. (288–0139). A downstairs café sticks to light and simple offerings, while the main restaurant is the domain of William Tell's highly imaginative owner/chef Peter Muller. Local ingredients are melded into new creations that conceptually are an outgrowth of the nouvelle movement. Reasonably priced lunches and dinners (about $10 and $15 respectively), or *à la carte.* Closed Sundays; dinner only Saturdays.

Vegetarian

Le Commensal, 2115 St. Denis (845–2627). More original and diverse than vegetarian restaurants normally tend to be, though the whole idea of salad that you buy by the pennies per gram is a little too post-hippie. Very inexpensive and pleasant, though. No credit cards.

Also, Indian restaurants and crêperies generally serve non-meat and non-fish dishes.

Vietnamese

Vietnamese restaurants are sprouting like, well, bean sprouts along Prince Arthur and Duluth primarily, but elsewhere as well. One of the mainstays, and an excellent one at that, is **Le Gout du Viet Nam,** 4157 St. Denis (842–0708). With its strong French influence, Vietnamese cooking differs markedly from the Chinese and Japanese styles with which most North Americans are familiar. Duck is used bountifully here, as are vegetables and seafood. A delicate cuisine, inexpensive, and presented in an atmosphere of great friendliness. Also, **Le Colombier,** 73 Prince Arthur (845–0502), offers five or six courses for $9–12.

Night Life

Montreal is a late-night city. Traffic starts mounting Thursdays about 10:00 P.M. around the Crescent and Ste. Catherine areas and doesn't let up until somewhere close to dawn. The same scene repeats itself Friday and Saturday nights, only the tie-ups get worse then. Most nightspots are open until 3:00 A.M., and Montrealers seem intent on taking full advantage.

Listings for night-life activity—theater, concerts, ballet, opera, jazz and rock clubs, floor shows—are contained in the bi-monthly magazine *Virus*, which unfortunately is published in French only, and in the Saturday entertainment section of the English-language newspaper *The Gazette*. *Montreal Scop*, distributed free in most hotels, also contains monthly listings for live events and some non-critical round-ups of goings on at hotel nightclubs and restaurants. The listings in *Scop* are about evenly divided between English and French.

Generally, Montreal's theaters and concert halls are closed during the summer, except for the one-night stands by this or that touring popster. But there is much outdoor entertainment to be enjoyed—and often for free. Each spring the tourist bureau publishes an extensive listing of summer events that includes performances by small opera and theater companies, puppet and marionnette shows, dance troupes, chamber ensembles, folk dancing, and pop concerts.

Prince Arthur Street and Place Jacques Cartier in Old Montreal are popular with street performers who pass the hat after their impromptu shows. Guitarists strumming and singing '60s folk favorites, stilt-walking flute players, mimes, magicians, bluegrass bands—all are part of the scene. And there are anonymous musicians galore in the Métro stations playing to help lessen the irritation of waiting for a train (which is never too long in coming anyway).

Jazz and film fans may wish to build their visits to Montreal around two internationally acclaimed festivals: Indoor and outdoor concerts—some on stages set up on the street—are part of the annual July **Montreal Jazz Festival** held in the St. Denis district. For schedules, write Montreal Jazz Festival, 416 Ontario St., Montreal H2L 1N6 (514–849–8321).

The ten-day **Montreal International Film Festival** is held in August. Film-makers and fans flock to this event, which is centered at Place des Arts and the Parisian Cinema on Ste. Catherine Street, but for which some screenings are given at other venues around town. Ticket books good for entry to multiple events are usually made available. For information: World Film Festival, 1455 Maisonneuve West, Montreal H3G 1M8 (514–879–4057).

Le Cinema Parallele, 3684 St. Lawrence Blvd. (514–843–4725), is a small year-round repertory movie house specializing in art films and those of historical value. Following the nightly screenings at 8:00 P.M. you can sip espresso and discuss things political and otherwise at Café Melies, a small coffeehouse out front.

See the daily papers for specifics about current English-language features.

Place des Arts, previously described in the Downtown section, is the city's cultural center in winter. Salle Wilfrid-Pelletier, with almost 3,000 seats, is home to **Les Grands Ballets Canadiens, L'Opéra de Montreal** (under Jean-Paul Jeannotte), and **L'Orchestre Symphonique de Montreal** (under Charles Dutoit). All three companies offer season subscriptions as well as single-event tickets. Major concert artists, be they Frank Sinatra or Montserrat Caballe, appear here. Concerts are also periodically given at churches around Montreal, and at theaters on both the Montreal and McGill University campuses.

The intimate 800-seat Theatre Port-Royal and the 1,300-seat Theatre Maisonneuve share the building next door to Wilfrid-Pelletier in Place des Arts. Theatre Port-Royal features an unusually wide stage (wider than that in Salle Wilfrid-Pelletier), concrete walls, and no provisions for hanging scenery; it is the base for the repertory presentations of Compagnie Jean Duceppe. Theatre Maisonneuve is a more traditionally executed space with orange seats, gray walls, and bronze-like ceiling. It is used for stage shows as well as some concerts.

Brochures listing the season's offerings for each of the above-mentioned companies are available directly from the Place des Arts box office: Place des Arts, Montreal 129 (514–842–2112).

The biggest pop stars headline the 20,000-seat Forum, 2313 Ste.-Catherine (932-6131), where the Montreal Canadiens hockey team plays in winter or, for the really big names, the Olympic Stadium (255-4400), where the Montreal Expos baseball team resides. Less well-known touring artists hit the Spectrum, near Place Des Arts (861-5851). A favorite rock club is **Club Soda,** 5240 Parc Avenue (270-7848), which features a good mix of up-and-coming local and out-of-town bands. A fun place in a slightly tacky neighborhood, Club Soda attracts the young new wavers. Ticket prices vary from about $7–$12.

Jazz fans have two main outposts throughout the year: **Biddle's,** 2060 Aylmer (842-8656), is the more mainstream. Centrally located downtown, this cozy but fairly good-sized room appeals to business types, young couples, and long-haired jazz fans alike. Charles Biddle, the proprietor/bassist who's often on stage, sets the tone with his distinguished good looks and three-piece suits, though the music is anything but stuffy and the barbequed ribs and chicken demand being eaten with your fingers. Big-name acts sometimes make their way on stage here, too. Music charge varies with the act (there's usually no extra fee at the bar).

Air du Temps, 191 St. Paul West (842-2003), in Old Montreal, is something of the prototypical jazz club—smokey, cramped and Bohemian—and is also the city's main bastion of new jazz. The headliners are mostly Canadian and local, but the quality is consistent. There's a cocktail hour from 5:00–8:00 P.M. weekdays, when solo pianists hold forth; Thursdays through Saturdays there's a $3 cover charge for sets that begin at 9:30 and go on until whenever.

A third jazz possibility is **Le Grand Café,** 1720 St. Denis (849–6955), though the singles scene is so stiff here that the music is really an afterthought.

Floor shows are available at a number of the larger hotels, including the Château Champlain's **Le Caf'-Conc** (878–1688), Bonaventure-Westin's **Le Portage** (878–2323), and the Queen Elizabeth's **Salle Bonaventure** (861–3511). Dinner with the show runs about $25 per person at each, with an additional cover charge at Château Champlain; alternately, there's a cover charge of about $10 for the show without dinner. (Add a high-priced drink or two to that charge). The aforementioned Charles Biddle also holds forth at **Les Voyageurs,** a lounge in the Queen Elizabeth, when not at his own club. **Le Sabayon,** 666 Sherbrooke West (288–0373), has a floor show with bellydancers, singers, and comedians along with a full Greek menu. All of the above appeal primarily to business travelers on company expense accounts.

Discos

There's something macabre about the whole notion of **Douze Twelve 34,** 1234 Montagne Street (861–0927), possibly the most "unusual" of Montreal's discos—formerly a funeral parlor, and still looking it on the outside. The young professional crowd gets all duded up for hanging out here. The doors open at 9:00 P.M. nightly, but no one serious about the singles life would dare to show up before 10:30. The doors close again at 3:00 A.M.

Discos virtually line Crescent, Montagne, and nearby Maisonneuve as well as lower St. Denis and, to a lesser extent, Ste. Catherine. The Crescent area is for the 30-and-over professional set. St. Denis has the leather-jacket crowd on the street while the clubs are for the young 20s to early 30s singles in neat but casual dress. Ste. Catherine, with its late night video game arcades and flashing lights, is for the 18–25ers. The major hotels almost all have spots for dancing, as well, though you won't find many locals at them. Of note as of this writing, but subject to the fast-changing and often whimsical preferences of their patrons:

Chez Brandy, 407 St. Jean Baptiste (872–9178), in Old Montreal, with a pleasant, non-jet-setty young professional and arts-oriented crowd.

Septembre, 2015A Montagne Street (849–4544). As a bar, Thursday's is probably Montreal's most popular every day of the week; Septembre similarly boasts a trendy regular crowd throughout the year.

Vol de Nuit, 14 Prince Arthur East (845–6243), has the prettiest bar on Prince Arthur, and a wonderfully relaxed and casual ambience. The lively crowd is mixed between couples and singles 25–40 in the professions and the arts.

Altitheque 727, 44th floor Place Ville Marie, Royal Bank Building (861–3511). Popular among out-of-town visitors because of the view it offers along with the singles rites, but also populated by young professionals working in the area and nearby McGill and Concordia College students. Décor, of course, resembles the inside of a jet.

Bars

As with discos, the popularity of a given bar rises and falls based on no particularly detectable criteria. Some, incidentally, have dancing, too. Like its restaurant and disco partners, the bar at **Altitude 727** has a good view of Montreal; so do the rooftop bars at the **Centre Sheraton,** 1201 Dorchester (878–2000); **Château Champlain,** 1 Place du Canada (878–1688); and **Regence Hyatt,** 777 University (879–1370).

Thursdays, 1449 Crescent St. (288–5656) is certainly *the* place to see and be seen if you want to know what the 30-plus professional crowd is up to in Montreal these days. The ceiling fans, the Tiffany glass lamps, the plants do nothing to dull the roar of those fighting to get their orders in at the bar or find out what the attractive person next to them does for a living. There is a disco downstairs.

Abacus 2, 2144 Mackay St. (933–8444), is considerably more subdued, though the attention to dress (if not the trendiness) and age range match those of Thursdays. Downstairs from the fancy Chinese restaurant of the same name, the *New York* piano room is the focus.

Bar Grand Prix, Ritz Carlton Hotel, 1228 Sherbrooke West (842–4212), is the poshest and most sedate of the city's piano bars, but a genuinely romantic setting nonetheless. This is for winding down *after* you've met someone new, or for easing into the night with someone you already love.

Sir Winston Churchill Pub, 1459 Crescent (288–0616) is the place to be on a summer's eve when there's a table available on the *terrasse*. Sees itself appealing primarily to the under 30 soon-to-be professional set.

Winnie, 1455 Crescent (288–0623) prides itself on picking up the Churchill Pub's "graduates."

Bishop Street south of Ste. Catherine has a host of American-style bars of which **Woody's** was the most popular at the time of this writing. Nearby, though sometimes empty when there are people cascading down the steps to Woody's: **Kazouzz, Christopher's, Hemmingway's** and a host of others that seem to change names and ownership with the seasons.

Daytrips

Downhill and cross-country skiing (more rigorous than that found in Mount Royal Park), and sailing, swimming, and golfing are within an hour's drive of Montreal by car or bus, with most of the best-known resorts no farther than an hour and a half. The Laurentian Mountains, as these wooded hills that peak at Mount Tremblant's 3,150-foot height are known, serve as many Montrealers' weekend getaway. For tourists, they are a way of getting a taste of the country even on an essentially city-bound vacation. The off-seasons can be deadly here, as there is little to do during the day, but for sports enthusiasts at the right time of year the Laurentians offer bountiful delights. (When asked what guests at one resort might do after breakfast one snowless March, the young keeper of the ski equipment, doing his schoolwork, looked up meekly and suggested, "Wait for lunch?")

The Laurentians, reached via highway Route 117 going north, are heavily wooded and brilliantly green. There are reportedly more than one hundred ski lifts, and easily hundreds of miles of cross-country trails in

DAYTRIPS *110*

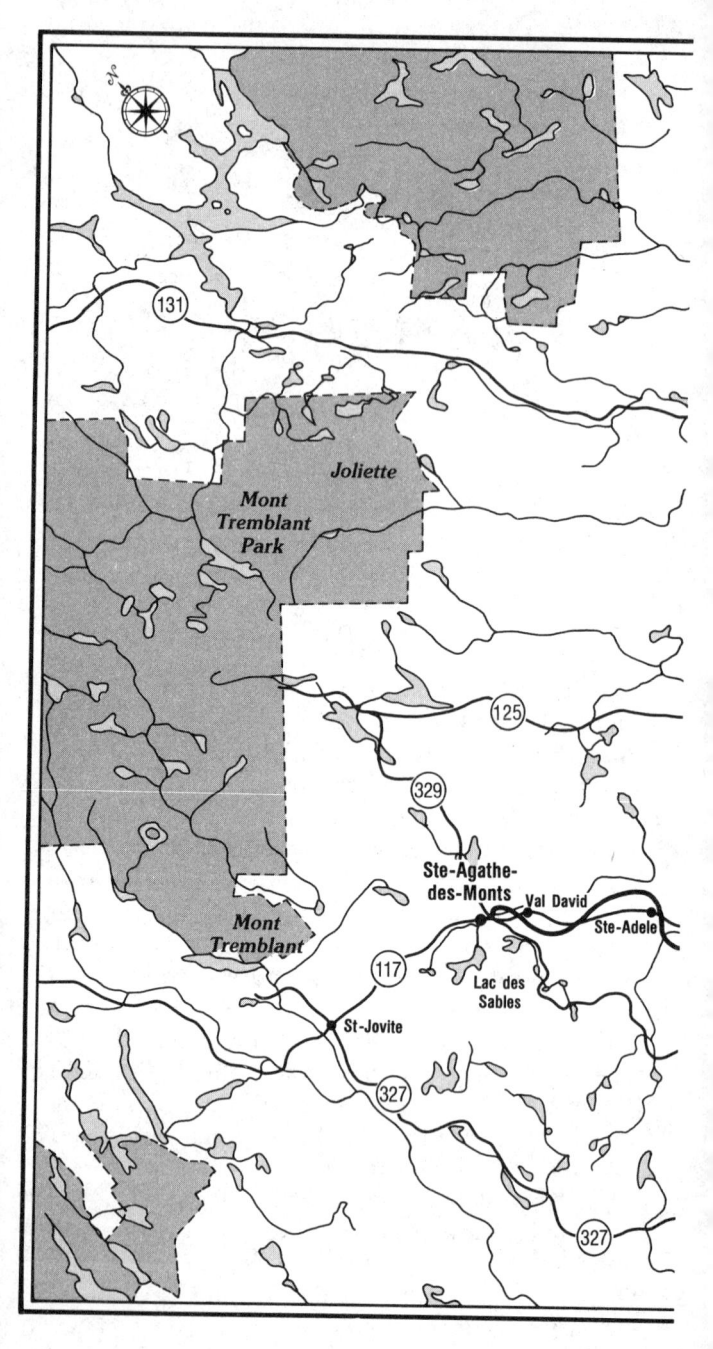

111   DAYTRIPS

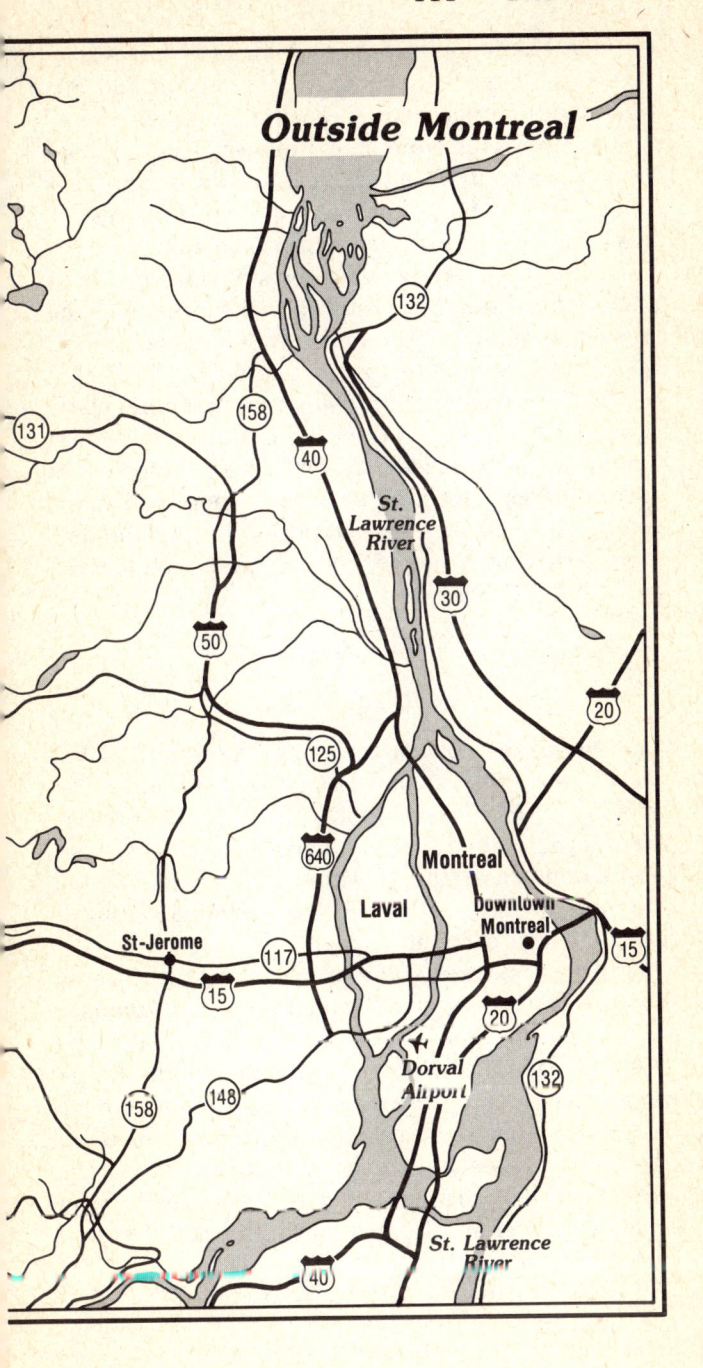

the area. Lakes dot the entire region, as do fine restaurants. The larger resorts at Mt. Tremblant and Ste. Agathe-des-Monts feature evening entertainment as well as everything from babysitting services to equipment rentals, at rates that include two meals a day along with a room. Motels along the main roads are less expensive, a little farther from the mountain, but leave you the freedom to dine where you will. Go as a full-fledged side trip or just for a day's ride. For the latter, the fifty-mile ride between St. Jerome and St. Jovite is the stretch to concentrate on.

Buses leave the central Montreal station regularly throughout the day for the 93-mile trip to Mount Tremblant (514–842–2281). Differently routed buses make different stops, so be sure to inquire ahead if you're going to, say, Val David or Ste. Agathe-des-Monts. Driving is simple, and the roads well marked and quickly cleared during snow season.

One of the nearest resorts, **La Sapinière** in Val David (Box 190, Val David PQ JOT 2NO; 819–322–2020; or in Montreal, 514–866–8262), is also recognized throughout Canada as one of the nation's finest. A one-hour drive from downtown, the hotel is set on the edge of Lake Sapinière. The secluded setting is nothing short of breathtaking.

In winter, when you look out from the 70-room hotel's outstanding glass-fronted restaurant, the lake sits frozen, the trees are strung with icicles, the surrounding mountains are blindingly white. Room prices include three meals a day, which is a little much given the classically heavy style of cooking that comes out of the kitchen and the fact that many items on the menu (which "changes" daily) are repeated from lunch to dinner and again at lunch the next day until they are gone.

Still, at an average $100 per day per person (double occupancy), this is both an excellent value and an outstanding place for relaxing or sporting. There are sitting rooms with roaring fires in the winter for Scrabble, chess, or reading; a game room with ping pong, video games and bumper pool; a bar with organist (making music suitable for the hard of hearing); heated outdoor pool; cross-country ski trails that double for hiking in summer; tennis, canoes, and a putting green. Downhill skiing is available at nearby Mount Plante.

The food is excellently prepared and makes use of fresh ingredients, though the hotel's availability for small business conventions seems to dictate a certain amount of coffeeshop filler alongside the pâtés, terrines, poached fish, and beautifully sauced meats. The chef, Marcel Kretz, is captain of Canada's Culinary Olympic Team and a gold-medal winner in his own right. Service is impeccable and there's an outstanding wine list. Complete dinners run about $20–$25; lunches are a bit less. Only the buffet-style breakfasts that sit atop burners for several hours leave much to be desired—though special requests for fresh eggs will be honored.

In addition to the hotel-style rooms in the main building, all with private bath and most with sitting area, there is a motel-like building across the street. La Sapinière also has a number of fully equipped cottages available for rent by the week, month, or season. Men are required to wear jackets to dinner, and, overall, the atmosphere is a little stiff for those seeking hedonistic excitement. Given its location so close to Montreal *and* to points farther north, however, La Sapinière can be a perfect stop for a two-day rest.

If you're passing through Val David with a family en route to another Laurentian stop, consider lunch or dinner at **Au Petit Poucet,** right on Route 117 (819-322-2246). The specialty here is maple syrup-smoked ham, which is served to many of the 400 or so diners the restaurant can accommodate at any given time. *A la carte* main dishes run to about $12, and while décor and service are nothing to write home about, the food is ample and hearty.

Those seeking more activity and a younger crowd than is the norm at La Sapinière should head either to **Station Touristique du Mont Tremblant,** Mont Tremblant PQ, JOT 1Z0 (819–425–2711), or to **Gray Rocks,** St.-Jovite, PQ JOT 2HO (819–425–2771). Both are full-service resorts where you ski right outside the door in winter or swim, ride horseback, or waterski in summer. At either, expect to pay $200 per couple, in season, including breakfast and dinner, and most services (lift tickets but not ski rentals, for example). The more popular, Mont Tremblant, charges $15 on weekdays and $20 on weekends and holidays for unlimited use of its 20 slopes and trails to those not staying at the hotel. Reduced rates are offered for full-week packages. Discounts for children vary.

Many motels and less grandiose lodges dot roads 327 and 117 nearby and the towns of Mont Tremblanc and Ste. Agathe-des-Monts. Some come with kitchenettes, suitable for family travel, while others boast almost total seclusion and a mere handful of rooms to help insure privacy and promote interaction among those guests who are booked in. Two possibilities among the latter establishments:

Chalet des Chutes, Mont Tremblanc PQ JOT 1Z0 (819–425–2738). Rooms with private bath in the motel wing are about $60 per night for two, about $40 in the chalet-like hotel where baths are shared. A piano bar is a late-night attraction for those staying and living in the area.

Auberge Sauvignon, Mont Tremblanc PQ JOT 1Z0 (819–425–2658). All of eight guest rooms (one with private bath), though the tiny dining room open to the public is the main draw.

Motels near the slopes run about $60 for a double during high season and go down in price (1) when snow fails to materialize and (2) the farther you get from the Mont Tremblant or Gray Rocks trails.

For additional sightseeing and eating:

Village de Seraphin (514–229–4777) is a recreation of a ninteenth-century village about 2½ miles north of Ste. Adele on route 117.

Boat rides are available on **Lake des Sables,** in Ste. Agathe-des-Monts, from mid-May through October (819–326–3656).

La Table Enchantée, Route 117 Lake Duhamel, St. Jovite (819–425–7113). Traditional Quebecoise cooking—meaty casseroles, head cheese, fresh snails —off-set by the occasional *nouvelle* effort. Dinners run about $12–$20.

Quebec City

From Montreal, it is about a three-hour trip by car or bus to the provincial capital, Quebec City. Here is an even more startling study in contrasts between old and new, in a city where French culture is clearly the dominating influence. English-speaking visitors, however, need not worry about being understood or understanding shopkeepers or restaurateurs. As anywhere, the effort to learn a few frequently used words in French will be duly rewarded; even so, those with no French in their vocabulary will have little difficulty, especially during tourist seasons when staffs all over are built up with bilingual students.

Winter trips to Quebec City should be timed, if possible, to coincide with the late February *Carnaval*. This ten-day festival of parades, ice sculpting, canoe races (on the largely frozen St. Lawrence!), and ethnic cuisine is a time of celebration akin to New Orleans' Mardi Gras, though you may need snowshoes to plow through it.

Summer is also a wonderful time, as artists and street performers fill the alleys of the Old City—particularly along Tresor Street in the Latin Quarter—and galleries, boutiques, and coffeehouses are open for late browsers. Early July finds an ambitious free jazz and folk festival staged outdoors at the theater next to City Hall.

The Old City, bounded by the fort walls first begun by Samuel de Champlain in the early 1600s, is where visitors will want to spend most of their time, regardless of the season. Within those walls, the Upper Town is where most of the historical sites, hotels, and restaurants are located. Place d'Armes is the main square off which Dufferin Terrace offers a promenade for strolling. At the center of the square is a statue of Champlain. Overlooking the St. Lawrence as it does, this is the starting point of any walking tour. The local tourist information bureau is also right off the square.

Château Frontenac Hotel, 1 Carriers Street, Quebec PQ G1R 4P5 (418-692-3861), is a major sight unto itself as well as the city's most beloved hotel. Construction on this castle-like structure located right off Dufferin Terrace commenced in 1893; renovation is an on-going process. Many of the 500 guest rooms have a view of the water (preferable to being over the square, which can get noisy at night), as do the bar and restaurant. Certainly there is no more convenient place to stay in the entire city.

The atmosphere is a little on the stodgy side—too elegant for a turn-of-the-century hotel in the throes of finding a comfortable balance between classicism and modernization. For a night or two, though, staying at the Frontenac may transport you back to another era, which easily atones for any stiffness. A room for two will run about $130, with weekend packages about $90 per person for two nights and ski week packages about $200 per person—both double occupancy.

QUEBEC CITY *118*

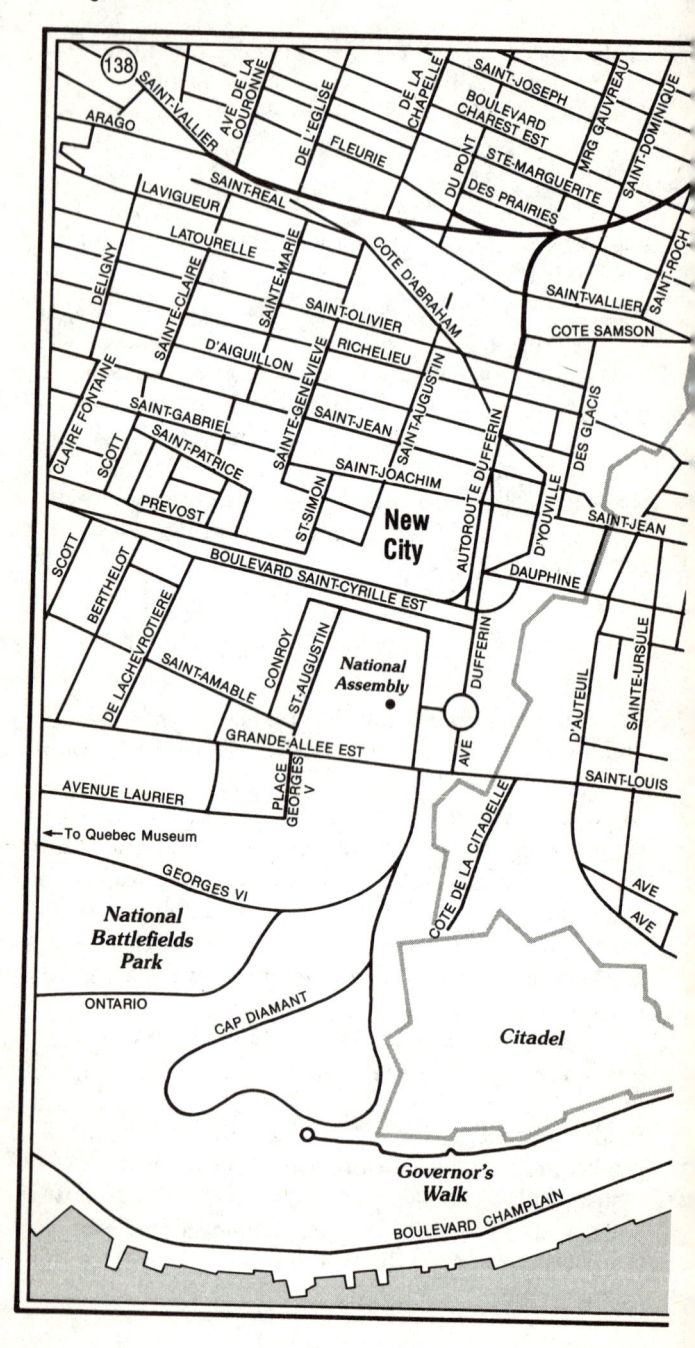

119 QUEBEC CITY

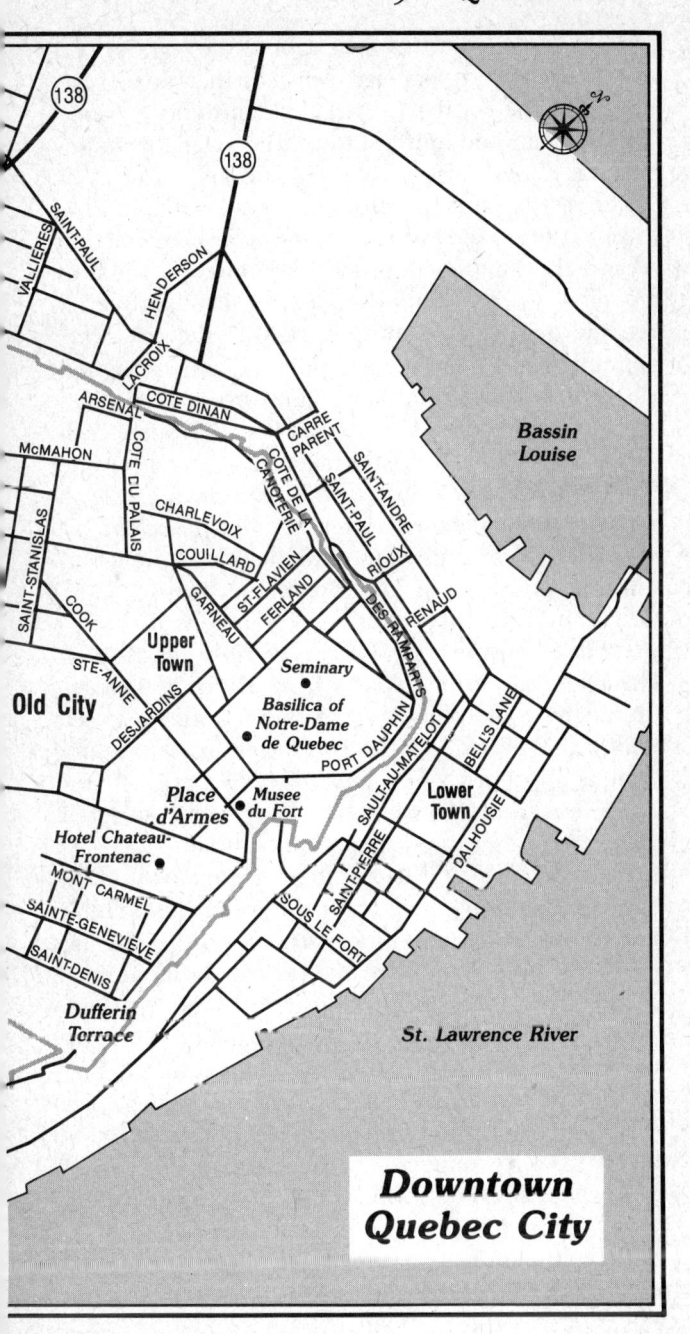

Downtown Quebec City

The Lower Town, at the foot of the cliff, is being restored to its original eighteenth-century style. Place Royale is the focal point of the renovation work, a market square no more but now the stage for numerous street performers. Inexpensive and moderately priced restaurants on the streets all around Place Royale cater to the local artists—who are beginning to inhabit the long-abandoned warehouses of the dock district—as well as to tourists. St. Paul Street has become the primary antiques strip in the city, while boutiques and galleries are popping up throughout the Lower Town. The restoration process is a slow one (detailed in photo displays at Fornel House, 27 St. Pierre Street) that will still take some years, but it is exciting to see the fabric of the area change.

The Lower Town is reached by *funiculaire* (50 cents), a one-car tram built onto the side of the mountain that lands you inside Louis Jolliet House. Jolliet House, built in the 1680s, unfortunately also has a tacky little souvenir stand that is terribly out of place. The *funiculaire* itself departs from Dufferin Terrace. Or, go by foot following the steep winding streets behind the Terrace or the Breakneck Stairs (yes, the name is appropriate) off *Côté de la Montagne*.

The Lower Town is in the process of great change, so singling out restaurants or shops is likely to be futile. Suffice it to say there are many, that the eighteenth-century architecture is often fascinating, that you can walk any of the streets safely, and that there are guided tours of the area daily in summer leaving from Soumandre House, at 29 Notre Dame Street, which serves as an additional branch of the tourist bureau. Call 418-643-6631 for information.

In winter, part of Dufferin Terrace is given over to a skating rink and toboggan slide. In summer, take the boardwalk promenade to the end in order to reach the flight of steps that will carry you up to Governors' Walk. This stroll, along the outer edge of the fortress walls, culminates at National Battlefields Park, just outside the Old City walls, and the Quebec Museum. The Park covers more than 230 acres and is an excellent place for picnicking. Also nearby is the Artillery Park. The museum (418-643-2150) is noted for its changing exhibitions of old and new works by Quebec artists.

The Citadel, near the St. Louis Gate and within the walls, was built between 1820 and 1832, and is still used for the Canadian army's lone remaining all-French regiment. Changing of the Guard takes place daily at 10:00 A.M. and Retreat is staged Tuesdays, Thursdays, and weekends at 7:00 P.M. Guided tours are available for $2 per person, though all of these activities are open to the public in summer only.

Château Bellevue, 16 Laporte Street, Quebec PQ G1R 4MR (418-692-3092), is one of several pleasant small hotels and rooming houses that line Governor's Walk and its nearby streets. This is the most modern of these establishments, with doubles about $70 a night; lodging at the rooming houses runs about half.

Off Place d'Armes, from which *calèche* rides ($30 per hour) can be taken, is Musée du Fort, a military history exhibit built around a light show and a scale model of Quebec City. Closed in December, performances are given regularly throughout the day the rest of the year. Next door is a Historical Museum of the city.

Basilica of Notre-Dame de Quebec, the Seminary, and the Seminary Museum are located at the foot of Tresor Street opposite City Hall. The cathedral, of course, is open throughout the year, though tours of the Seminary and the museum are available during June, July and August only. The Ursuline Convent and Museum, with access from Parloir and Donnacona Streets, respectively, are part of a school for Indian and French girls started in 1639. The Museum is open to visitors daily except Mondays. St. Louis Street features the oldest houses in Quebec.

Hotel Clarendon, 57 Ste.-Anne Street, Quebec PZ G1R 3X4 (418–692–2480), is a good alternative to Château Frontenac given its location across from City Hall, its prices (about $75 for a double), and its aspirations. Also the subject of non-stop up-grading, the Art-Deco lobby and restaurant are magnificent (though service in the restaurant borders on neglect). Presumably the clash between Art-Deco and Victorian influences in the guest rooms will one day be resolved. Indeed, the rooms seem to be undergoing renovation bit by bit. The bar in the lobby features live entertainment and an active singles scene among locals of college age. The hotel is casual if anything.

Perhaps the most fun way to dine in the old part of Quebec City is to walk the streets reading menus, peeking in the windows and seeing how the crowd and the food look. That's hardly a foolproof method of determining where to dine, but the quality of restaurants in the Old City is exceptionally high.

Café de la Paix, 44 des Jardins Street, Quebec G1R 4L7 (418–692–1430), "1,000 feet from the Château Frontenac," offers the perfect balance between outstanding French cuisine and an atmosphere that is bright, lively, and suggests that eating should be *fun*. The fare, concentrating on seafood, is lighter than classical but heartier and more ample than is the norm for *nouvelle*. The waiters, mostly Greek and Italian, are unusually friendly and encourage you to take your meal at your own pace—no matter how long the line at the door is. Reservations are a good idea even in off-season. The check for two, with a liter of house wine, 10% meal tax, and 15% tip will come to about $75 for a meal that will be long remembered.

The heaviest concentration of better restaurants

in the Old City is along St. Louis Street, and right off its sidestreets. As at Café de la Paix, there are special lunches at most that run $10 and under for three courses. **Aux Anciens Canadiens,** 34 St. Louis (418–692–1627), with its waitresses in native costumes and hearty Quebecoise cuisine, makes the most of its setting in the 1675 Jacquet House. Fixed-price lunches and dinners are emphasized—about $8 for lunch, $20 for dinner.

Meal times generally are 11:30 A.M. to 2:30 P.M. and 6:30 to 10:30 P.M. Less pricey alternatives to those above are the bistros of the Lower Town and the creperies that dot the entire area. Also popping up increasingly are croissant shops serving these light, multi-layered buttery rolls filled with cheese, sausage, mushrooms, or any variety of sandwich foods.

The New City offers both turn-of-the-century Victoriana in some neighborhoods, skyscrapers and high tech in others, and much that falls between—houses and office buildings of the 1930s and 1940s, for example, and fast-food chains that almost seem a mysterious presence. The National Assembly Building, a Renaissance-style structure in which the Quebec Parliament meets, is one sight near the Old City St. Louis Gate on Grand Allée. Guided tours are run daily during the summer; weekdays most of the rest of the year. For departure times call 418–643–7239. Almost across the street is the National Battlefields Park and the Quebec Museum discussed earlier. The Grand Theater, used for concerts, ballet, opera, and drama, is a striking structure worth visiting either for a performance or for a tour. (Check the daily newspapers for event listings.)

The New City is also brimming with sparkling new modern hotels. **Auberge des Gouverneurs,** 690 Blvd. St.-Cyrille East, Quebec PQ G1R 5A8 (418–647

–1717), probably tops the list—high-tech but not unduly cold, with year-round outdoor heated pool, sauna, excellent if high-priced restaurant, and bars. Double rooms will run about $110, though weekend tourist packages are commonly available when booked in advance. Both the Auberge and the nearby **Hilton International Quebec,** 3 Place Quebec, Quebec PQ G1K 7M9 (418–647–2411), are but a few minutes' walk to the Old City's Kent Gate entrance. Doubles at the Hilton cost about $10 more than at the Auberge. And both the Hilton and the **Loew's Le Concorde,** 1225 Place Montcalm, Quebec PQ G1R 4W6 (418–647–2222), have rooftop bars, Le Concorde offering piano music and full restaurant service at L'Astral while the Hilton's Eden turns into a disco in the evenings. Le Concorde also has year-round indoor and heated outdoor pools. Doubles cost a little less than at the Auberge—and you are considerably farther from the Old City walls. Motels are concentrated at the western entrance to the city, a fair distance from the Old City.

The New City of course has restaurants all over, but there is a particularly great concentration of them, representing classical French, Quebecoise, Italian, Greek, and other ethnic cuisines, on Grande Allée just a block or two west of the National Assembly Building and within walking distance of the hotels mentioned above. If none is exceptional, all are expert, friendly, and not overly formal—typical of Quebec's pride in the ability to balance attention with food and ambience. Most also have room for at least a few outdoor tables in summer.

Night life is concentrated in the Old City, with numerous cafés, bars, and discos. As in Montreal, the popularity of any given establishment waxes and wanes, but Quebec City is not a stop on the jet set's itinerary. Hang-outs tend to be dominated by those of college age, less so at the hotels because of the prices.

Excursions from the City

The Laurentian Mountains extend eastward from Montreal, and Quebec City-ites have their own resorts for skiing and swimming. To the north is Lac Beauport, serviced regularly in winter by a ski-bus that leaves from major hotels, and no more than a half-hour away. It is at the heart of a three-mountain range very popular among Quebec downhill skiers: Mont St. Castin, Le Relais, and Stoneham. Cross-country trails are nearby at Club du Mont Tourbillon and Manoir du Lac Delage (418–848–2551). For day trippers, lift tickets can be purchased daily; there are also week-long passes and ski-week packages offered by Quebec City hotels.

Manoir St. Castin, PQ G0A 2C0 (418–849–4461), is a Lac Beauport resort with full sporting facilities no matter the season, the top-rated of the resorts in the area. You can expect to pay as much as $150 for two during high season, including two meals a day, though there are numerous weekend and full-week packages available that cost half (and less) as much. Also on the lake is **Auberge Normande,** 161, Tour du Lac Rd. (418–849–4486), where prices and facilities are less extravagant.

Perhaps the most popular area for both downhill and cross-country skiiers is Mount Saint Anne Park, east of Quebec City. This, too, is an easy day trip, though a number of motels and lodges are clustered around nearby Ste. Anne de Beaupre. The latter town is site of Montmorency Falls, a waterfall whose drop

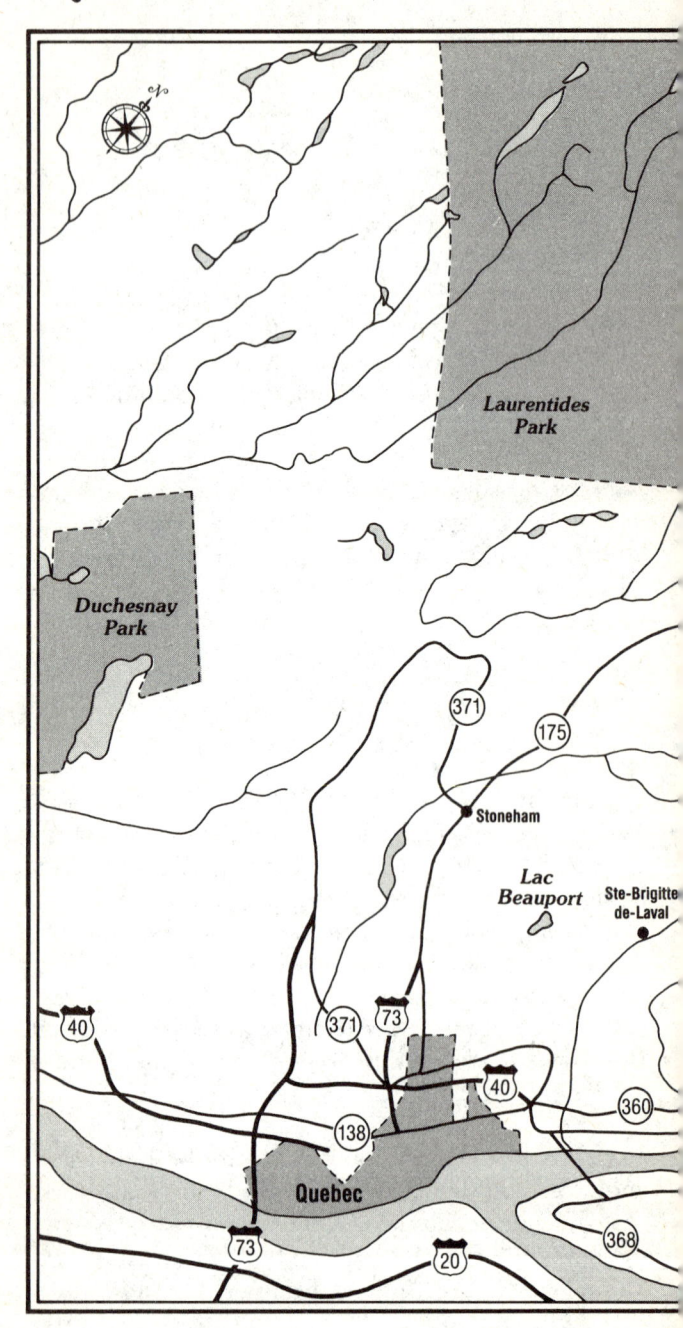

QUEBEC CITY 126

127 QUEBEC CITY

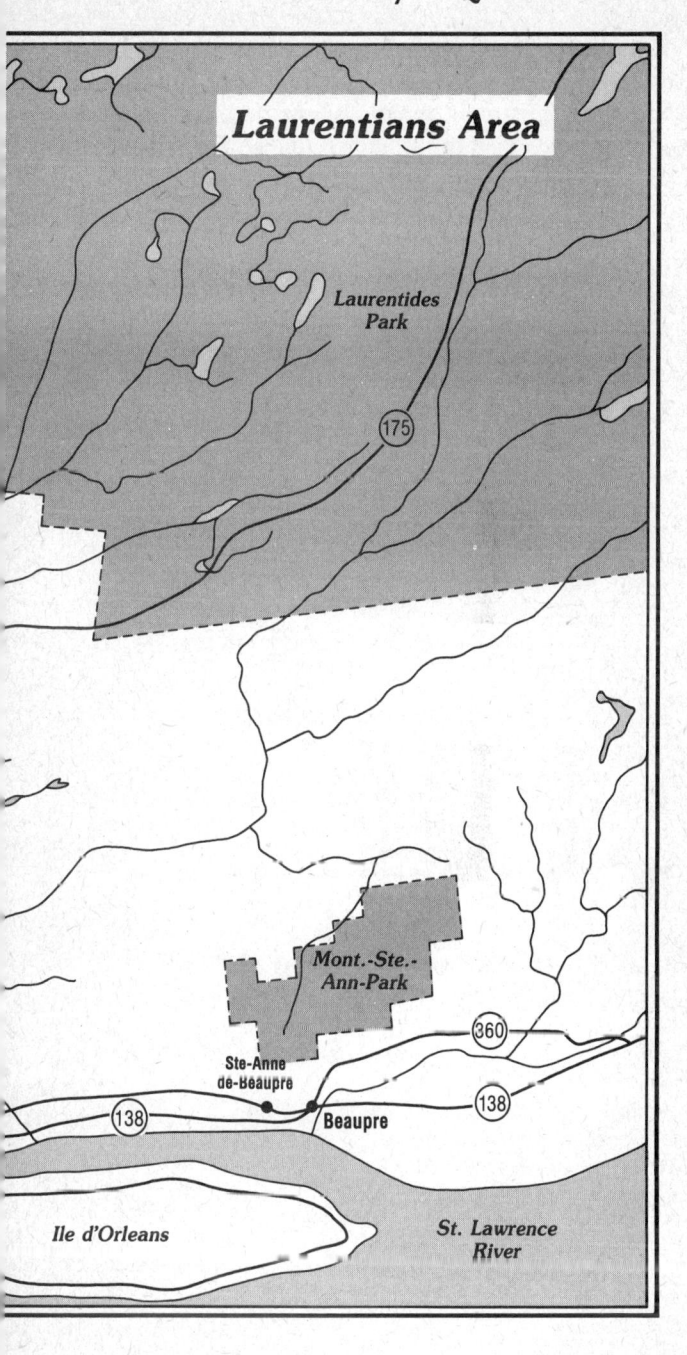

Laurentians Area

Laurentides Park

(175)

Mont.-Ste.-Ann-Park

(360)

Ste-Anne-de-Beaupré

(138) Beaupre (138)

Ile d'Orleans

St. Lawrence River

is longer than that for Niagara Falls. The park itself has two dozen lifts and trails. Ile d'Orleans, an island in the St. Lawrence, is a pleasant strip of farmland that can be fun to visit in summer, when strawberry-picking is in season or just to see the vegetable gardens in full bloom.